The lake at Studley Royal.

Shire County Guide 3

NORTH YORKSHIRE AND NORTH HUMBERSIDE

Cyril Bainbridge

Shire Publications Ltd

CONTENTS

 First published 1984, second edition 1989. Shire County Guide 3. ISBN 0 85263 987 2.

Set in 8 point Times roman and printed in Great Britain by C. I. Thomas & Sons (Haverfordwest) Ltd, Press Buildings, Merlins Bridge, Haverfordwest, Dyfed.

ACKNOWLEDGEMENTS
Photographs are acknowledged as follows: Cyril Bainbridge, pages 3, 6, 20, 26, 28 and 51; Geoffrey Wright, page 53; York Department of Tourism, page 45. The rest, including the cover, are by Cadbury Lamb. The map on pages 62 and 63 is by D. R. Darton.

COVER: *Gordale Scar.*
BELOW: *Hunmanby church.*

Aysgarth Falls, Wensleydale.

1
The landscape

A more exciting mixture of contrasting countryside scenery and rich historical heritage than that of North Yorkshire and North Humberside could not be found anywhere in Britain. The scenery has a rich variety, mountainous uplands and three famous high peaks (to say nothing of the lesser ones), vast moorland tracts inhabited by sturdy breeds of sheep, limestone fells of the Dales and Pennines, rolling hills of the Yorkshire Wolds, rushing waterfalls and surging streams that expend themselves and become lazy rivers meandering through thickly wooded valleys. The coastline extends for more than 100 miles (160 km) and presents an equally varied seascape. Each part of the region has characteristics of its own but unlike some other areas the different aspects are not always easily defined into specific areas: one merges gently into another with an amount of overlap.

The vastness of the region, together with the growth of motorways and the building of the Humber Bridge, makes it accessible to most other parts of England: its sheer size often makes tours within it longer than the original journey to get there.

Wherever one goes there are reminders of the region's significant role in British history — in the castles and ruined abbeys, the stately homes and vast estates, the sites of hilltop settlements and burial mounds, the ancient travel routes that originated before roads were constructed and still criss-cross the moors and, in the Dales, the old 'green roads' across the moors and fells, originated by bronze and iron age people and now much frequented by hikers.

Much to the disgust of many of its residents, the term 'riding', which had been used since Viking days to describe the administrative divisions of Yorkshire, was rendered redundant in the local government re-organisation of 1974 and boundaries were changed, the old East Riding being mostly absorbed into the new county of Humberside. So resentful were several local councils at this new designation — Beverley, Holderness and North Wolds in particular — that they reinstated the name of East Yorkshire into their titles. The area covered by this book is the new county of North Yorkshire and the part of Humberside which used to be in Yorkshire.

CHAPTER 1

THE COAST

The coastline of North Humberside and North Yorkshire stretches from Spurn Point in the south to the little fishing village of Staithes in the north.

The Spurn peninsula is a thin spit of barren coastline, 3½ miles (6 km) long, which is rich in flora and fauna, especially birds. There is little human life here, apart from lighthouse keepers, coastguards, courageous lifeboatmen and wardens of the nature reserve of the Yorkshire Naturalists' Trust, which bought it in 1960. But the quiet of the thin spit of land contrasts with the wildness and menacing character of the North Sea.

The lifeboat station has been here since 1810 and is the busiest in Britain, with a long list of rescues and bravery awards to successive members of its crew. They are one of the few crews to operate full time, living with their families in a group of dove-grey detached cottages built around a courtyard near the coastguard station.

The peninsula has been built up by the action of the sea shifting sand and clay from coastal erosion further north. Its own survival is tenuous: it is constantly under threat from the sea and the lifeboatmen and others whose necessary work keeps them there live in almost constant danger of being cut off.

The nature reserve attracts many migrating birds and is one of the most important bird observatories in Europe.

Northwards beyond the peninsula are several small resorts, such as Withernsea and Hornsea (see chapter 10). The coastline from Spurn Head to just south of Bridlington is the longest stretch of boulder clay coastline in Britain. The low cliffs are constantly eroding and whole villages have been lost to the sea over the past three centuries, as well as valuable acres of agricultural land.

Bridlington, Filey and Scarborough, with their long stretches of clean sands, are the favourite coastal haunts of Yorkshiremen. The coastal scenery here has changed to white chalk cliffs, out of which juts Flamborough Head. Around Bridlington is a good place to watch gannets: their main nesting site in England is near here at Bempton, which also attracts many other forms of bird life. The chalk cliff colonies are supervised by the Royal Society for the Protection of Birds.

Further north, from Scarborough to Staithes, the coastline continues with dramatic cliffs and steep roads twisting down to quaintly picturesque fishing villages. Beyond Whitby, Boulby Cliff at 666 feet (202 m) is the highest cliff in England. The Cleveland Way runs the length of this 30 mile (50 km) stretch of the coast.

The Yorkshire coastline is one of great variety: fine, clean sands, changing coastal scenery, dramatic seas and fascinating bird life, not to overlook the man-made pleasures of its popular holiday resorts.

HOLDERNESS

Inland, the Holderness area is flat and fertile agricultural land. By contrast with other parts of North Humberside and North Yorkshire, it is not an area of scenic beauty, although there are many charming villages and some fine country houses. One of its attractions, however, is its legacy of impressively large churches, many of them big enough to be mistaken for cathedrals. Stones carried down from Scotland during the ice age or rolled across the seabed from Scandinavia are said to have been used in their construction. The fine interiors of these churches and country houses reflect the prosperity of the rich merchants and farmers who built them.

Holderness is triangular in shape, bounded by the Wolds, the North Sea coast and the Humber estuary — an area of low-lying plain and some of the finest agricultural land in Britain. Some of the farms are of huge proportions, extending to nearly 1,000 acres (400 ha). Oats and barley are the main crops. They gently quiver in the summer breeze, but in winter cold east winds blow across the flat landscape.

THE WOLDS

The flatness of the Holderness plain gently merges into the green slopes of the Yorkshire Wolds, which seem almost mountainous in comparison with the evenness of the plain. But, however deceiving the change, the green hills never even approach a height of 1000 feet (300 m).

The Yorkshire Wolds stretch in the shape of a crescent from the coast at Filey, curling southwards to the Humber at North Ferriby, west of Hull.

The scenery here is of rounded and gently sloping hills, prolific with wild flowers. Unspoilt villages abound but there is no town of any great size, apart from two on the borders with Holderness: Beverley, which rises dramatically from the surrounding lowland, and Great Driffield. The western boundary is near Pocklington.

The Wolds are extensive, 60 miles (100 km) long and between 5 and 15 miles (8 to 24 km) wide. In summer the ripening grain crops give the landscape the appearance of having a thick-piled golden carpet. Dotted about are the beautifully landscaped parklands of some of the county's finest country houses, such as Burton Agnes and Sledmere House (see chapter 7).

There is much sheep farming and horse breeding in the Wolds. It was here that the enclosure of agricultural land was first carried

Bempton Cliffs.

out in the eighteenth century and famous bloodstock stables were established.

THE PLAIN OF YORK

The Plain of York divides the Yorkshire Dales and Pennines from the North Yorkshire Moors to the north, the Wolds and the flat Humberside country to the east and south. This, again, is rich agricultural land, intersected by the Great North Road, which now frequently bypasses the several fine old towns with ancient and hospitable coaching inns. Boroughbridge, Thirsk and Northallerton, the administrative capital of North Yorkshire, are all situated within the northern area of the Plain. It stretches northwards from the borders of South Yorkshire like a huge pointing finger, 60 miles (100 km) long, 12 miles (20 km) wide at its narrowest and 30 miles (50 km) at its broadest near York. It reaches north almost to the Tees.

The Hambleton and Cleveland Hills provide vantage points from which to view the extensive vista of flat land, its hedges giving a chequer-board effect to this landscape of mixed farming.

Several valleys converge on the Plain, such as the Vale of Mowbray and the Derwent valley around Malton, and there are many country estates within its borders, the finest being Vanbrugh's elegant extravaganza at Castle Howard.

Also within the Plain are the sites of many of the great battles of English history, including Stamford Bridge, Towton and Marston Moor (see chapter 9).

One of the finest landscape views in England is that from the top of Sutton Bank, between Thirsk and Helmsley, from which the wide expanse of the Plain is seen unfurling below.

THE NORTH YORKSHIRE MOORS

The moors of North Yorkshire extend from the Plain of York to the sea, divided from the Wolds to the south by the vale of Pickering, which stretches from the coastal cliffs of Scarborough and Filey to the Howardian Hills in the west. They consist of some of the finest moorland in Britain, the highest parts clad in heather, and are enriched by a number of small yet colourful dales with small villages providing active centres of rural life. They form the North Yorkshire Moors National Park.

The high moors are lonely country, inhabited almost solely by hardy breeds of sheep, pheasant and grouse. Here the enthusiastic walker must be an insular as well as an insulated character for he will probably trudge for many miles and for many hours without meeting a fellow human. But, given the right weather, he will be rewarded with spectacular scenery, particularly of the formation of the

Janet's Foss, near Malham.

lower valleys.

The less energetic visitor will find the valleys and woodlands more attractive than the high moors. The largest of these dales is **Farndale,** renowned for its colourful display of wild daffodils in the spring and for the river Dove which flows gently through the dale. Through **Bilsdale** goes one of the few main roads in the moors, that from Helmsley to Teesside. **Ryedale** contains some of the finest scenery and ancient buildings such as Rievaulx Abbey. Further east are **Bransdale,** wilder than its neighbouring dales, the attractive sounding **Rosedale, Newton Dale,** a narrow but deep gorge that runs from the Esk valley to the Vale of Pickering, and **Thornton Dale,** with its much photographed thatched cottages.

The northern parts of the dales and moors are within easy reach of Whitby. Near the border with Cleveland, encircling these upland areas, are the Cleveland Hills, which stretch down to Osmotherley, where the Hambleton Hills take over as a dividing line between the moors and the Plain of York and Yorkshire Dales to the east.

A landmark of the northern moors is Roseberry Topping, an isolated hill which appears to reach higher than its 1000 feet (300 m). This is Captain Cook territory: he spent his boyhood at Great Ayton, where there is a Cook museum in the schoolroom he attended and a prominent monument on nearby Easby Moor.

Water from the high moors east of Roseberry Topping runs into the Esk, which cuts through its own dale to Grosmont and on to Whitby, the only Yorkshire river between the Tees and the Humber to flow directly into the North Sea. North of the Esk are several other small and narrow dales — Westerdale, Danby and Glaisdale.

THE YORKSHIRE DALES

The Yorkshire Dales vary in their size, appeal and character. The chief dales are Wensleydale (one of the few to be named after a place rather than a river), Nidderdale, Swaledale, Wharfedale, Ribblesdale and Airedale (much of which is now in West Yorkshire) but there are many smaller dales.

Most of the Dales are within the 680 square miles of the Yorkshire Dales National Park, which was created in 1954. Nidderdale, however, is not included. Almost all of this national park is within the county of North Yorkshire. The larger dales are diverse in their topography: Swaledale is narrow, steep-sided and wild, Wensleydale broad and wooded, Wharfedale long and winding, and Ribblesdale has vast rolling moorland between mountainous uplands.

Swaledale. Swaledale, the most northerly of the larger dales, is famous for its sturdy breed of sheep, which graze in huge flocks throughout the year on the wild and lonely higher slopes of the dale. Wool was the foundation of the dale's prosperity, and that of many of the religious houses which before the Dissolution of the Monasteries owned vast tracts of moorland. The river from which the dale takes its name drops dramatically down a number of spectacular waterfalls to reach the richly wooded lower end of the dale. Lead mining, relics of which abound, was another contributor to the growth and prosperity of the dale, of which Reeth is the 'capital'.

Wensleydale. Wensleydale is the largest of the Yorkshire Dales and although it has a river flowing through it, the Ure, it derives its name from the village of Wensley. Hawes is the main town of the upper dale, around which the scenery is wildly spectacular. Leyburn lies in the centre. Masham is in the heart of the lower dale, which is green and fertile. Several smaller dales branch off the main dale. Within Wensleydale are some spectacular ruined castles and abbeys and picturesque waterfalls such as those at Aysgarth. It was the monks from Jervaulx Abbey who originated Wensleydale cheese, made from ewes' milk, and which became a farmhouse industry.

Wharfedale. One of the larger dales, Wharfedale extends north of Ilkley, with its Roman associations, and is an area of superb scenery varying from picturesque river views to limestone fells and high moors. The dale begins in Langstrothdale in what was once forest land, includes Buckden, the very name of which conjures up hunting scenes, and extends down the Wharfe valley with grey limestone terraces on either side. One of the most attractive stretches of river is around Bolton Abbey and Barden Tower.

Ribblesdale. Ribblesdale is a popular area for walkers, potholing enthusiasts and railway enthusiasts, for the huge Ribblehead Viaduct spans the dale, carrying the Settle to Carlisle line across the mountainous moorland, dominated by the great bulk of Whernside, the highest of Yorkshire's Three Peaks. The quarrying of limestone is a leading and often disfiguring industry in the dale. The river Ribble flows westwards into Lancashire.

Nidderdale. The upper reaches of Nidderdale are the gathering grounds for several great reservoirs which have created a lakeland landscape in the dale. The dale and the river Nidd from which it takes its name drop down to Pateley Bridge and on to Knaresborough, through a thickly wooded gorge overlooked by the ruined castle.

Arkengarthdale. This is a wide, grassy and exposed dale running northwards off Swaledale from Reeth and bears many scars of

Castle Bolton, Wensleydale.

the old lead mining industry. Arkle Beck flows through it to reach the Swale.

Colsterdale. This is a small, quiet dale from which various becks and the river Burn flow into the Ure below Masham. This dale extends for 12 miles (19 km) along the course of the Burn.

Coverdale. One of Wensleydale's offshoots, Coverdale has steep and winding roads from which there are spectacular views into neighbouring Wharfedale. The river Cover flows into the Ure below Middleham. Thirteenth-century Coverham Abbey (chapter 5) is within the dale, which was the birthplace of Miles Coverdale, translator of the Great Bible.

Littondale. This flat valley, from which limestone fells climb steeply, is a branch of Wharfedale, with the shadow of Penyghent at its head. It is a former hunting forest which the monks of Fountains Abbey developed as sheep grazing land.

Malhamdale. One of the most popular tourist centres, Malhamdale is a narrow, limestone dale with Malham Cove, Malham Tarn and the spectacular Gordale Scar as its main attractions.

CHANGING LANDSCAPE

Demand for water by the industrial cities of West Yorkshire, erosion by the sea in some coastal areas and afforestation have all had a part in altering the traditional landscape during the twentieth century. Agriculture, which is one of the main industries of the small dales, still rotates between grassland and crops, and sheep farming remains traditional in the upland areas but there have been changes in animal husbandry in the lower valleys with dairy farming now frequently becoming the dominant form of agriculture. In recent years there has been some diminution of hedgerows, small woodland and copses as a result of changes in agricultural methods. The National Park authorities have predicted that a quarter of the hedgerow trees in the park might disappear as a result and to offset this loss farmers are being encouraged to plant trees in rough or unproductive agricultural land.

In the Dales in particular there is a noticeable and traditional absence of hedgerows to divide the land. The divisions here are provided by drystone walls, which extend in their chequer-board pattern for miles across the hills and dales and represent thousands of man hours in their erection. The art of drystone walling is one that is disappearing and, while some repairs are still carried out by the remaining practitioners of the art, it is now often easier and cheaper to use wooden fencing.

LONG DISTANCE FOOTPATHS

Three of the long distance paths managed and maintained by the Countryside Commission are within Yorkshire and North Humberside: the Pennine Way, the Cleveland Way and the Wolds Way.

Long distance paths can be used for an occasional day's walking over a relatively short distance but, whether they are used in this way or walked in their entirety, caution and commonsense are required. Maps are necessary, particularly for the high level stretches, which are often devoid of prominent landmarks; an ability to use a compass is also necessary and sensible footwear and clothing are essential. Apart from an occasional day's walking and the stretches of coastal path, careful planning of the itinerary should be undertaken. Those who are prepared to camp en route should remember that many of the pathways are across private property and permission needs to be sought from the landowner before pitching tents.

The Pennine Way. This was the first of the long distance paths to be created, in 1965. It is also the longest and for the most part is arduous and strenuous, traversing some of the most remote areas of Britain, much of it wild and exposed stretches of moorland. Having begun at Edale in the Peak District of Derbyshire, the Way passes through West Yorkshire and Craven before entering the Yorkshire Dales north of Gargrave. Within the Dales it crosses Malhamdale and from Penyghent drops to Horton-in-Ribblesdale, then proceeds across moorland fell to Hawes, Abbotside Common and the high Great Shunner Fell (2340 feet; 713 m) to reach Thwaite, skirt Keld and cross Stonesdale Moor on its way northwards to Northumberland and over the Scottish border to its conclusion at Kirk Yetholm.

The route takes ancient tracks and old drove roads as it traverses the moors. It is a challenging but spectacular walk and one to be undertaken by experienced walkers since, except in a few instances, there are long distances between stops, little opportunity to pick up transport and often unpredictable and quickly changing weather. Walkers, even those with experience, are advised not to attempt to cross the exposed moorland stretches alone.

The Cleveland Way. This follows an ancient track used since Roman times and its route is almost entirely within the North Yorkshire Moors National Park. It begins at Helmsley and takes a circuitous route along the Hambleton and Cleveland Hills to reach the coast, just outside the area of the national park, at Saltburn-by-the-Sea. This section is 54 miles (87 km) long. It then closely follows the coast,

Gordale Scar.

either by clifftop or at sea level to Scarborough and on to Filey — a further 45 miles (72 km) — where it links up with another long distance walk, the Wolds Way.

Although less arduous than the Pennine Way, the Cleveland Way includes some strenuous and high moorland paths that can be hard going even for the experienced walker. The coastal section is easier but subject to the vagaries of the coastal weather.

The Wolds Way. This long distance path was opened in 1982. It begins at Filey and follows a circuitous route through the chalk hills of the Yorkshire Wolds to reach the Humber at Hessle Haven. The Way takes a low-level route through agricultural land, crossing some of the prettiest and most characteristic East Yorkshire scenery.

The Lyke Wake Walk. This was started in 1955. Those who succeed in completing within twenty-four hours the 40 mile (64 km) course over moorland and bog from Osmotherley across the North Yorkshire Moors to Hackness, near Scarborough, are rewarded with membership of the Lyke Wake Club.

Three Peaks Walk. This is another challenge to the serious walker, with membership of the Three Peaks of Yorkshire Club for those who manage to reach the summit of all three peaks in one day, a minimum of just over 20 gruelling miles (32 km). Twelve hours was at one time regarded as a reasonable time for the course but this has been whittled down by several hours. Walkers taking up the challenge are, for their safety's sake, asked to sign out at the Penyghent Cafe in Horton-in-Ribblesdale before starting. For the really fit and hardy there are now also races in the spring for foot walkers and one in the autumn for cyclists, although the terrain is such that they have to carry or push their machines for at least 5 miles (8 km) of the course.

WATERFALLS

Aysgarth. North Yorkshire and the Yorkshire Dales in particular are richly endowed with magnificent waterfalls. Among the most scenic are those at Aysgarth in Wensleydale, where the previously placid river Ure suddenly rushes into a rocky gorge and changes into a wild and foaming torrent as it drops down a series of wide limestone shelves. The magnificence of the upper fall can be observed from an old packhorse bridge under which the river flows before reaching the equally spectacular middle and lower falls downstream. After the violence of these falls, the river resumes its serene course through Wensley and Masham.

Gordale Scar. Another impressive waterfall is Gordale Scar, just over a mile from the village of Malham. The twin falls of Gordale Beck as they plunge from the flat land around Malham Tarn down the deep chasm of Gordale Scar afford a dramatic sight that has been recorded in picture and prose by many famous artists and writers.

Overhanging walls of limestone rock reaching a height of over 400 feet (120 m) form a huge gorge, down the centre of which the beck plunges. At one time the gorge was a huge cave, containing the waterfalls, the roof of which collapsed years ago. The beck eventually joins the river Aire south of Malham village. Janet's Foss is a smaller but also impressive waterfall nearby.

Hardraw. A mile or so north-west of Hawes is the hamlet of Hardraw — and another spectacular sight. Through the Green Dragon inn the visitor has access to a footpath leading down a ravine to Hardraw Force, the highest single-drop waterfall in England. The water appears from an overhanging rocky lip and pours down the 100 foot high (30 m) fall. A pathway at the bottom of the rock goes behind the waterfall just above the foot of the drop. Along the glen is a large natural amphitheatre, the acoustic qualities of which are suited to the music of brass bands. For fifty years until 1929 many of the leading northern brass bands took part in contests here which attracted thousands of spectators. Contests have been revived in recent years.

Hardraw Force.

Ingleton. The rivers Twiss and Doe converge on Ingleton through valleys and glens and down spectacular waterfalls before combining as the river Greta. Through the valley and the glens is a dramatic 4 mile (6 km) walk, which has been made less arduous by the erection of footpaths and bridges, although it can be heavy going after rain. Two hours is an average time to complete the walk up one valley, across a stretch of moorland and down the other valley. By the upward route, the Twiss flows down a succession of smaller waterfalls until Thornton Force is reached at the head of the glen, where the water falls a dramatic 40 feet (12 m) into a large pool in a natural amphitheatre. The return by way of the Doe valley is through more thickly wooded gorges.

Kisdon Force. High up in Swaledale at the village of Keld are several waterfalls, or 'forces' as they are often named. Kisdon Force, a short distance from the village, is regarded as the finest in the dale.

THE FORESTS

There has always been much woodland in North Yorkshire, although the original forest areas declined with the clearances for agriculture and animal grazing. The big estates of the eighteenth and nineteenth centuries were landscaped and well wooded but the setting up of the Forestry Commission in 1919 brought widespread organised afforestation. There are now more than 46,000 acres (18,600 ha) of national plantations in the area and a further 15,000 acres (6100 ha) of privately owned woodland. The two main forests are based on Pickering and Helmsley.

Many forest roads have been opened to visitors in North Yorkshire under the management of the Forestry Commission to provide forest drives which vary in length from 14 miles (23 km) to about 50 miles (80 km). There are plenty of car parks and in some places picnic areas are also provided. Several public roads run deep into the forest areas but two forest drives make use of toll roads inside the forests.

One drive, which at its start provides excellent views across the Vale of Pickering, is picked up near the attractive village of Thornton Dale, 3 miles (5 km) from Pickering. From the village square, keep left at the first fork, and after ¾ mile (1200 m) through a deciduous wood and along a level stretch of road, with magnificent views on the left of Newton Dale and Rosedale, a road on the right marked 'Low Dalby only' is taken. The drive through the forest is then by a toll road, some of which is narrow and twisting and requires careful motoring. In the village of Dalby there is a forest information centre and a small museum has been set up in old farm buildings. There are numerous parking places and attractive picnic areas along the route.

The other drive runs from the former station at Levisham, north of Pickering, through Newton Dale to Mauley Cross, where the main road back to Pickering via Stape and Newton-upon-Rawcliffe is regained.

The Forestry Commission has devised a number of tours based on Scarborough, Pickering and Helmsley, taking in the forest drives, details of which are contained in a guide book, published by HMSO.

Pickering.

LAKES

Hornsea Mere. 2 miles (3 km) long and a mile (1.6 km) wide, this is Yorkshire's largest freshwater lake. On its shores and small islands can be found many species of rare flowers and the numerous varieties of birds that nest there provide much interest for ornithologists. There are other attractions on the mere, such as sailing and boating, for the pleasure-seeking visitor.

Malham Tarn. The second largest lake in Yorkshire, Malham Tarn forms part of the Malham Tarn Estate, a National Trust property and a nature reserve. The nearby house, which is not open to the public, is now a field studies centre where residential courses for students are held. It was formerly the home of Walter Morrison, a rich bachelor, who numbered Charles Darwin, John Ruskin and Charles Kingsley among his friends. Cars are not admitted but there are no restrictions on cyclists and walkers — indeed, a section of the Pennine Way passes the Tarn — and there is a nature trail around the estate. The lake is ½ mile (800 m) in diameter.

Semerwater. After Hornsea Mere and Malham Tarn comes Semerwater, a popular lake now much used for sailing and water skiing, particularly at weekends. It is reached along narrow country roads from Bainbridge in Wensleydale. Three streams flow into the lake and England's shortest river, the 3 mile (5 km) long river Bain, issues from it. It lies in the hollow of the surrounding hills and there are several ancient settlements on its borders. There is a circular walk from the village of Bainbridge via Countersett, around the lake and back through Stalling Busk.

CAVES AND POTHOLES

The action of water penetrating the underlying rock in the limestone areas of the Yorkshire Dales has created a complex honeycomb of caves and potholes, some with spectacular underground waterfalls and stalactite and stalagmite formations. The exploration of potholes is a pursuit of the expert members of caving and potholing clubs and requires much specialist equipment, to say nothing of courage, as will be apparent from the dramatic rescues which frequently have to be undertaken. There is an abundance of caves and potholes in the area of the Three Peaks, particularly around Ingleton.

Alum Pot. On the edge of Ribblesdale near Selside, this is said to be the most impressive pothole in Britain.

Gaping Gill. This pothole on Ingleborough has a sheer 265 foot (81 m) drop into a huge chamber underground.

Hull Pot. One of two pots on the side of Penyghent, this is now an enormous open cavern, 300 feet (91 m) long and 60 feet (18 m) deep, since its roof fell in many years ago. Nearby are the much smaller Calf Holes, 30 feet (9 m) deep.

Ingleborough Caves. A pleasant 1 mile (1.6 km) woodland walk from the village of Clapham leads to the caves. The walk is a nature trail through the Ingleborough Estate, which has an 8 acre (3.2 ha) lake. There are guided tours of the caves, which are rich in interesting geological formations.

White Scar Cave. On the road out of Ingleton to Hawes, this cave runs ½ mile (800 m) under Ingleborough. Here there are underground lakes and waterfalls and electric lighting effects display the stalactites and stalagmites in a variety of colours.

Stump Cross Caverns. On the Grassington to Pateley Bridge road, these are a series of caves of varying sizes with stalactites which have been given imaginative names. One, called appropriately The Cathedral, has stalactites resembling the pipes of an organ, which play musical notes when struck. Here again, clever use of electrical effects displays the unusual formations in a colourful fashion which enhances their magnificence.

OTHER NATURAL FEATURES

Brimham Rocks. Between Ripon and Pateley Bridge, Brimham Rocks are another unusual feature of the North Yorkshire landscape. They are an outcrop of millstone grit which, ravaged by wind and rain, has been naturally sculptured into fascinating and often grotesque shapes and figures and given appropriate names.

The Buttertubs. Buttertubs Pass is the road which links Hawes in Wensleydale with Muker in Swaledale. It is a road from which there are breathtakingly spectacular views and at the summit is a series of deep shafts in the limestone rocks, named The Buttertubs, now lined with ferns and regarded as one of the minor wonders of Yorkshire.

The Hole of Horcum. This is another spectacular sight, a natural hollow north of Pickering, near the A169 Whitby road, which has become popular as a centre for hang-gliding.

Heather thatch at Grassington.

2
Folklore, customs and traditions

Yorkshire pudding, brass bands, cricket and singing are among the more familiar traditions and customs associated with Yorkshire and Humberside, but there are many other old customs, not so well known, that are still observed.

There are brass bands elsewhere in Britain but Yorkshire was one of the places where they originated and it would be difficult to convince a Yorkshireman that there are better bands elsewhere. The records are in his favour, for the contest results over the years show the predominance of bands from Yorkshire in the winning positions at championships.

Continental cookery may have penetrated to Yorkshire and nowadays there are many chic restaurants but the demand for good plain fare is still met and a substantial Yorkshire high tea of ham off the bone, with or without chips, is an experience not to be missed. And there is more than a chance that you will have your Yorkshire pudding served in the traditional manner — not as a small, round, soggy concoction surrounded by roast beef and vegetables but as a separate course in its own right with a covering of gravy.

Cricket is a subject which occupies many an evening's discussion in the pub and would provide enough material for several volumes.

Singing in Yorkshire is comparable with the same pastime in Wales. Male voice choirs abound, as well as choral societies, and performances of Handel's *Messiah* in public halls, churches and village schoolrooms are an annual ritual. The performances are usually amateur but the standards are invariably high.

The area's strong agricultural associations are reflected in the many popular agricultural shows and gymkhanas that are held annually. One of the largest is the **Great Yorkshire Show** at **Harrogate** in July. Many of the shows in the Dales, **Kilnsey Show** for example, have exhausting fell races associated with them. That at **Burnsall** is claimed to be the oldest fell race in Britain.

In the agricultural centres there are regular sales of cattle and sheep; it is a fascinating experience to visit these sales and to observe the colourful country folk who attend and to listen to the foreign-sounding language of the auctioneers and the comments and conversations of the farmers, many of whom are from remote moorland farms. The market at **Hawes** in Wensleydale is one of the most interesting; in the imposing market hall there more than a hundred thousand sheep and lambs and twelve thousand head of cattle are sold every year.

Many customs are centuries old and some have Scandinavian origins, like the sword dances performed at the **Plough Stots Service** at **Goathland,** near Whitby, every January. The 'stot' of the title was the local name for a bullock and was transferred to the young men who dragged a plough in the ancient processions. Nowadays dancers brandishing 30-inch (760 mm) swords perform the dances originally brought to the area by Norsemen more than a thousand years ago.

Some of the customs are performed regularly while others are infrequent celebrations. Every evening at 9 o'clock for example, an ancient **horn-blowing ceremony** is enacted in **Ripon.** It dates from the days before Ripon had a mayor, when the chief official of the town was known as the Wakeman. One of his daily tasks was the sounding of a horn to mark the setting of the watch, which announced to the inhabitants that the town was in the care of the Wakeman for the night. The town's motto, 'Except ye Lord keep ye cittie, ye Wakeman waketh in vain', is inscribed on the town hall in the Market Square and the horn blower, wearing a three-cornered hat, sounds his horn at each corner of an obelisk in the square.

Another type of horn-blowing ceremony takes place daily at 9 p.m. from the time of Holyrood (27th September) until Shrove Tuesday at **Bainbridge** in Wensleydale. The ancient forest of Wensley embraced the entire valley to the Westmorland border and in Norman times was a wild forest area used for hunting by the sporting lords of Middleham. The custom of blowing the horn was intended to guide travellers in the surrounding countryside to the safety of the village. On still, quiet nights the horn has been heard as far as 3 miles (5 km) away. When not being blown the horn hangs in the entrance hall of the Rose and Crown public house, which has been catering for the needs of travellers for more than five hundred years.

The **York Mystery Plays** are among the oldest and most famous of the traditional ceremonies of Yorkshire. They date from about 1340, a series of medieval religious plays that were originally written and performed by the ancient craft guilds of the city. There are forty-eight plays, which together tell the whole Bible story: they vary in length from eighty-six to 545 lines. The plays have been adapted for modern audiences from the original old English. The traditional performances were on special wagons which would stop at points throughout the city. They are now enacted every four years over a four week period as

Richmond Castle.

part of an arts festival. Performances take place in front of the ruins of St Mary's Abbey in the Museum Gardens.

Another of the less frequently celebrated customs is that of **Beating the Bounds** at **Richmond**, which takes place only every seven years (1990 is the next celebration).This custom dates from Elizabethan times or even earlier when the town burgesses, jealously guarding their rights and privileges, toured the precincts and limits of the borough. The modern celebration is a colourful occasion, with a procession headed by the banner bearer and followed by civic officials and other dignitaries, starting off their perambulation in the morning from the town hall. Claims and proclamations are made along the way, with stops for refreshment and sports, the whole affair lasting into the evening.

Most of the customs, however, are celebrated annually, around the same time each year. Some are religious in character, like the **Feast of St Wilfrid** which is celebrated at **Ripon.** St Wilfrid is the patron saint of Ripon Cathedral and every year on the Saturday preceding the first Monday in August a procession is held to celebrate St Wilfrid's return from exile in 686. Its original date is unclear but the procession has been held for hundreds of years. The Feast of St Wilfrid originated in a charter granted to Thomas, Archbishop of York, by Henry I in 1108. It permitted a fair for the four days of the feast in April. The modern celebration, now lasting a fortnight, takes place in July and August, with the procession as the centre piece.

Planting the Penny Hedge, a ceremony which takes place at **Whitby** every May, dates from 1159, when a wild boar, hotly pursued by hounds, found refuge in the chapel and hermitage at Eskdaleside, which was at that time occupied by a monk from Whitby Abbey. The irate huntsmen set upon the monk when they discovered he had closed the doors on the hounds. On his death bed he is reputed to have implored the Abbot of Whitby to spare their lives provided they and their successors did penance by building every year a hedge of stakes and branches at the edge of the sea strong enough to withstand three tides 'without removing by the force of the water'. The penny hedge ('penny' is a corruption of 'penance') is planted each year, tides permitting, at 9 a.m. on the eve of Ascension Day on the east side of the upper harbour near Boyes' Staith, Whitby.

Many of the customs are of a sporting nature. One of these is the **Kiplingcotes Derby**, held every year at **South Dalton**, North Humberside, on the third Thursday of March. The course, which goes through several parishes, is said to be the first racecourse to have been laid out in Britain and the race is claimed to be the oldest in the world. The first race was in 1519 and it was run at intervals for the next hundred years until two local squires invested a sum of money to ensure it was run annually. Any inclination by the leaders to hold back a little is understandable since the winner receives a lesser reward than the runner up. The former receives the interest on the investment, usually about £5, while the latter gets the stake money.

Another sporting occasion is **Kilburn Feast**, usually held during the second week of July, when all manner of unusual sports — terrier racing, grass track racing, an open quoits match in the village square — are held to the accompaniment of barn dances and other entertainments.

It was in the village of **Kilburn** that Robert Thompson, a manufacturer of fine furniture, adopted the custom of marking all his products with a small carving of a mouse. Through this practice he became known as the 'Mouse Man'.

Outdoor games were held in medieval times to celebrate Shrovetide, a period given over to revelry before Lent. These are still observed at **Scarborough** each year in the annual **Skipping Festival**, the origins of which are uncertain. But skipping in the roadway is apparently an ancient right which modern exponents exercise, nowadays in competition for road space with motorists along Foreshore Road.

Another annual custom in Scarborough is the **Sounding of the Pancake Bell** on Shrove (or Pancake) Tuesday. The bell hung in the former St Thomas's Hospital and was used night and morning as a curfew signal, but on Shrove Tuesday it was rung at noon to warn housewives to start preparing the traditional pancakes. When the hospital was demolished the bell was removed to one of the local museums but the traditional ringing on Shrove Tuesday has been maintained.

Some of the celebrations are now mere remnants of their ancient counterparts. All that now remains of a former seven day horse and cattle fair at **Seamer**, near Scarborough, is an annual procession and reading of the 1383 charter at various points in the village, at the end of which the Lord of the Manor throws coins to assembled schoolchildren.

Other old customs concern produce of the land. The annual **Old Gooseberry Show** at **Egton Bridge**, near Whitby — 'Old' refers to the history of the show rather than the age of the produce — has been held for over 150 years and is open to any grower in Britain provided he becomes a member of the Egton Bridge Old Gooseberry Society. The exhibits are gooseberries of many varieties, some of them incredibly large.

In the **First Fruits of the Harvest** ceremony at **Richmond**, the first local farmer to present a respectable sample of the season's wheat is given a bottle of wine by the Mayor, who has led a colourful procession from the town hall to Trinity Tower. The successful farmer then traditionally invites the assembly to drink to the mayor. His original prize does not go far, but he does receive a second bottle for subsequent consumption at home.

In a county with strong connections with the sea it can be expected that mariners will figure in some of the old customs and ceremonies. St Hilda, Abbess of Whitby, was the patron saint of fishermen and many churches are named after her. An annual service at St Oswald's church, **Flamborough**, on the Sunday of the second week in October is dedicated to the **Harvest of the Sea**; it is a fishermen's thanksgiving service which includes the singing of fisherman and lifeboat hymns and the church is decorated with crab pots and fishing nets.

Fairground folk and showmen assemble in Hull for a week every October for **Hull Fair**, the largest gathering of its kind in Britain, which has been held every year since the charter was granted in the fourteenth century.

The horn-blowing ceremony at Ripon.

CHAPTER 2

DIARY OF EVENTS

January

Plough Stots Service, Goathland, near Whitby, Plough Monday (first Monday following 6th January).

February

Ringing of Pancake Bell, Scarborough, Shrove Tuesday.

Shrovetide Skipping Festival, Scarborough, Shrove Tuesday.

March

Kiplingcotes Derby, South Dalton, North Humberside, third Thursday.

May

Planting of the Penny Hedge, Whitby, Ascension Eve.

June

East Coast Vintage and Veteran Car Run, Hull to Bridlington, second Sunday.

SSAFA annual air display, RAF Church Fenton.

July

Scorton Gold Cup Archery Tournament, Scorton, near Richmond, third Sunday.

Kilburn Feast, second week in July.

Masham Steam Engine and Fair Organ Rally, third Saturday.

Great Yorkshire Show, Harrogate, second Tuesday, Wednesday and Thursday.

St Wilfrid's Feast, Ripon, last week in July, first in August.

Harrogate International Festival of Music and Arts, July/August.

August

Whitby Folk Festival, week before late Summer Bank Holiday.

Annual Cricket Festival, Scarborough, August/September.

Rudding Park Horse Trials, Rudding Park, Harrogate, August/September.

Royal Yorkshire Yacht Club Regatta, Bridlington.

Burnsall Sports and Fell Race, third Saturday.

Egton Bridge Old Gooseberry Show, first Tuesday.

Burning the Bartle, West Witton, near Leyburn (burning the effigy of a legendary local outlaw), Saturday nearest 24th August.

September

First Fruits of Harvest ceremony, Richmond, date variable.

Nidderdale Agricultural Society Show, Beverley Park, Pateley Bridge, last Monday.

October

Hull Fair.

Harvest of the Sea Service, St Oswald's church, Flamborough, Sunday of second week.

Staithes.

3
Archaeological sites

Although both North Yorkshire and North Humberside are rich in archaeological evidence, few sites are formally open to the public. One of the main reasons for this is that, because the economy of the area has in recent centuries depended heavily on arable agriculture, the abundance of field monuments has been reduced through ploughing and many sites are now visible only as cropmarks and have been recorded by aerial photography. The majority of sites, too, are on private land and inaccessible by public footpath.

PALAEOLITHIC (before 4000 BC)

Many of the contours of the landscape originated at the time of the ice age when melting ice and snow from the moorland hills poured on to the lower ground, scouring out spillways and overflow channels and leaving mounds of debris behind them. The oldest archaeological site in the area of the North Yorkshire Moors is near **Kirk Dale** (SE 678856), where quarrying in 1821 revealed a cave containing bones and teeth of pre-glacial animals. Another cave, Victoria Cave at **Langcliffe,** near Settle, has provided evidence of palaeolithic man, who hunted in the hills and valleys after the ice age.

NEOLITHIC (4000-2300 BC)

Of the neolithic period, or new stone age, there are to be seen a group of long barrows, long oval hills of stone and gravel which were used for burials. Some of the best examples are at **Ayton East Field** (TA 000864) and **Kepwick** (SE 492904), within the North Yorkshire Moors National Park. There is a circular earthwork of the period at **Castle Dykes,** near Aysgarth.

BRONZE AGE (2300-700 BC)

The bronze age left behind a large number of small cairns and burial mounds, large barrows and several stone circles. The small cairns are often found on moorland ridges. Some of the more striking examples are to be found at **Allan Tops** (NZ 828028), about 6 miles (10 km) south-west of Whitby, where there is a group of about seventy-five cairns; **Danby Rigg** (NZ 710065), 1½ miles (2.5 km) from Danby village, where there are a large number of cairns and the remains of a burial mound; and **John Cross Rigg** (NZ 905025) on Fylingdales Moor, where there is another large group.

Stone circles were built by bronze age people and are thought to have played an important part in their rituals. Among the main examples are those at **Blakey Topping** (SE 873934), 7 miles (11 km) north-east of Pickering, where three stones about 6 feet (1.8 m) high are still in position; the **Bride Stones** (SE 576978) on Bilsdale Moor; **Danby Rigg** (NZ 708065), where a stone 5 feet (1.5 m) high is the only survivor of a circle that was once 42 feet (13 m) in diameter; **Flat Howe** (NZ 855046), a round barrow with a circular kerb of stones on Sleights Moor; **High Bride Stones** (NZ 855044), 5 miles (8 km) south-west of Whitby, where there are the remains of two circles, each of which has three stones still standing and others that have fallen; and **Standing Stones Rigg** (SE 983969), 6 miles (10 km) north-west of Scarborough. All these are within the North Yorkshire Moors National Park.

Elsewhere, there are stone circles in the Yorkshire Dales near **Yockenthwaite** and at **Bordley** on the east of Malham Moor.

Burial chambers of this period, known as barrows, are also to be found. Examples within the Dales are at **Askrigg** and **Bainbridge.**

IRON AGE (700 BC to AD 43)

The most northerly site of the earliest iron age people was at Castle Hill, **Scarborough,** where pottery of the late bronze and early iron ages has been found in rubbish pits beneath the foundations of Roman buildings. Sites of iron age villages and hillforts abound in various parts of the Dales and North Yorkshire Moors. A good example of an iron age village is at **Lea Green,** near Grassington, a site which was occupied from 200 BC to AD 400. Excavations at one of the hillforts have disclosed iron age pottery at **Boltby Scar** (SE 506857), near the Hambleton Hills, where a 2½ acre (1 ha) semicircular area also contains three barrows, one with an urn burial, of an earlier period than the fort. Another fort belonging to the second century BC is at **Roulston Scar** (SE 514816), ¾ mile (1.2 km) from Sutton Bank.

ROMAN (AD 43-410)

York. York stands out for the quality and quantity of its Roman remains. The city was one of the settlements of the Brigantes, the tribe which occupied the north of England, and the Roman governor of Britain, Quintus Petillius Cerialis, set off from Lincoln in AD 71 to conquer their territory. His temporary base camp where the Ouse and the Foss met became the permanent fortress of **Eboracum** when the Brigantes had been subdued.

A civilian city grew up outside the fortress

and became one of the main cities of the Roman Empire, visited by several emperors. It was used by Hadrian as the base for his campaigns further north. When the Emperor Constantius Chlorus died there in 306 his son Constantine, who was to become known as Constantine the Great, was proclaimed Emperor of Western Rome while in York.

The minster stands on the site of the Roman principia, the military headquarters, relics of which have been discovered and are displayed in the Undercroft museum. There are substantial fragments of the original wall that surrounded the Roman fortress, together with sewers and hypocausts of the period.

Cawthorn Camp (SE 785901). 5 miles (8 km) north of Pickering. This was a temporary camp occupying part of the ridge between Newton Dale and Rosedale.

Wade's Causeway. Running north-east from the camps at Cawthorn to the river Esk at Grosmont, in parts this is one of the best preserved Roman roads in Britain. Its line is clear for about 5 miles (8 km) from Cawthorn over Pickering and Wheeldale Moors: south-west of Goathland (SE 806979) a 1 mile (1.6 km) original section has been preserved by the Department of the Environment.

Wade's Causeway at Goathland.

Other Roman roads. Many of the Roman roads were taken over by the turnpikes and are now important main roads. An example is the Hawes to Ingleton road through Ribblehead, now noted for its railway viaduct; another is the Richmond to Lancaster turnpike.

There are other Roman roads around the village of Bainbridge, where there was a Roman fort. One of these roads ran from Bainbridge to another Roman settlement at Ilkley, and parts of this can be seen as a green track along the lower edge of Buckden Pike in Wharfedale.

Aldborough. This small town a mile (1.6 km) east of Boroughbridge, was known to the Romans as *Isurium Brigantium.* Many of the relics of its Roman occupation have been excavated and are displayed in the Roman site museum (chapter 8). Of particular interest are the tessellated pavements which have been preserved. Chapel Hill here is thought to have been a Roman burial place and Studforth Hill a Roman theatre.

Coastal signal stations. By the middle of the fourth century raids by Saxon pirates were troubling the Romans, coinciding with inland raids from Scotland. As a result old defences were rebuilt, including a series of five signal stations between the estuary of the Tees and Filey Bay. Each consisted of a watchtower of timber or stone, faced with a protective wall, and more protection was provided by a wide ditch. One of the survivors of these stations, on Castle Hill, **Scarborough,** is now in the care of the Department of the Environment and is well displayed, although part of it has fallen victim of cliff erosion. Another at **Goldsborough** (NZ 835151) is similar in its design to that at Scarborough but is built on Scarth Hill, a quarter of a mile (400 m) from the sea. This, too, is in the care of the Department.

VIKINGS

Excavations at **York** have revealed much information and many artefacts relating to the Vikings. They form the basis of a modern presentation in the Jorvic Viking Centre, a museum opened in 1984 on the site of an original Viking quarter in Coppergate (see chapter 8).

Elsewhere, other important monuments to this period of early history are the carved stone crosses that remain to be seen. **Kirkdale** church, on the borders of the North Yorkshire Moors National Park, has some fine Viking grave slabs and an inscribed sundial erected a decade before the Norman Conquest.

4
Castles

Much of the history of Yorkshire, indeed of England, can be gleaned not from history books alone but from the visible evidence of past centuries provided by its old buildings. Yorkshire has a valuable legacy in this respect. Many of the buildings are now in the care of government and other agencies; yet others are still in possession of families whose ancestors built them centuries ago. Almost without exception they have connections with royalty and other people who have played their parts in English history. The many castles in Yorkshire provide a rich source of material for the serious history student and their picturesque settings are a delight to the visitor. Castles derive from the Norman period, having been built as military strongholds for kings or feudal lords. The eleventh century was a period of much activity in the construction of castles. The general pattern was for an artificial mound of earth, or motte, surrounded by a ditch. It was surmounted by a palisade, and a courtyard, or bailey, would be attached to the mound. This original motte and bailey type is still in evidence in North Yorkshire at Pickering, where the motte remains, and in Holderness, where Skipsea Castle is another example begun soon after the Conquest.

Barden Tower, Skipton, North Yorkshire. 2 miles (3 km) north of Bolton Abbey.

Barden Tower has a fascinating history. Its name means 'valley of the wild boar' in Anglo-Saxon and it was originally built in the centre of hunting country as one of a number of lodges occupied by those who tended the valuable game and timber of the forest. It was a colony within the forest, with a formidable array of officials such as the verderer, the regarder or surveyor, the agister, who supervised cattle and other animals which came for pasture in the forest, and the woodward, who looked after the timber. Forest courts were held there to deal with offenders against the forest laws.

It came into the possession of the Clifford family in 1310 along with the rest of the Craven estates, but it was not occupied by the family until 1485, when Henry Clifford, who was known as the Shepherd Lord, made it his home. He earned his title through having spent the early years of his life hidden with shepherds on the Cumberland fells during the Wars of the Roses. Probably because of his upbringing he preferred the more modest Barden to the opulence of Skipton Castle not far away, although by all accounts his life at Barden was far from austere. He enlarged the Tower and built the chapel at the nearby Priest's House, which is now a farmhouse.

After his death in 1523 the tower reverted to use as a hunting lodge or temporary home for successive generations of the Clifford family until the advent of Lady Anne Clifford, who had it restored from its then ruinous state after she acquired the Craven estates in the mid seventeenth century. She often stayed there between her visitations to her extensive estates. Lady Anne must have had an acquisitive streak in her character since her determined occupancy of the tower deprived her niece, Elizabeth Clifford, of her rightful ownership. On Lady Anne's death in 1676 her niece took possession and through her it has descended to the Dukes of Devonshire, who still own it.

The tower was complete until the latter years of the eighteenth century, when roof timbers were sold and the building fell into disrepair. The outer walls have since been repaired to make them safe and the remains have become one of the most picturesque sights of a beautiful dale.

In 1982 the trustees of the estate converted a traditional Dales barn at Barden into a bunkhouse providing basic overnight self-catering accommodation for twenty people in bunk rooms for two to eight.

Bolton Castle, Castle Bolton, Leyburn, North Yorkshire.

Fleeing from Scottish rebels, Mary Queen of Scots accepted the dubious protection of Queen Elizabeth I, who placed her in the custody of the sixth Earl of Shrewsbury. She spent the next fourteen years in captivity in various parts of Yorkshire, being moved around to circumvent the many plots and counter-plots that were hatched to obtain her release.

One of the castles in which she spent part of her captivity was Bolton Castle, in the village of Castle Bolton, in which she was imprisoned from July 1568 until the following January. It was built in the late fourteenth century and was associated with the Scrope family, which provided many distinguished statesmen, lawyers and clerics. Richard Scrope, the first Lord Scrope, who was Chancellor of England, had the castle built.

The castle has been untenanted for over three hundred years and was dismantled after it capitulated in a siege by Parliamentary forces in 1645. An earlier Duke of Bolton who married into the Scrope family became owner of the castle but he and successive dukes lived not far away at Bolton Hall at Wensley. The castle has, however, been well cared for. It occupies a high standing position and the exterior is largely complete. In the ruined interior there is still some evidence of Queen Mary's bedroom and more up-to-date exhibits, including a reproduction of a nineteenth-century Dales kitchen, are displayed in a museum.

Clifford's Tower, York.

The stone tower was built in the thirteenth century to replace the Norman wooden keep which had been destroyed by fire during anti-Jewish riots in 1190. William the Conquerer had originally built a wooden fortress on an artificial mound on either side of the river Ouse. The existing tower was damaged during the siege of York in 1644. It was restored but seriously damaged again in 1684 when an explosion destroyed the roof. It is one of the few existing castle keeps of quatrefoil shape. Above the gateway is a chapel and a walk round the top of the walls presents fine views of the city and its historic buildings.

Gilling Castle, Gilling East, York.

Gilling Castle is at the western gateway to the Vale of Pickering. It was built by Roger de Mowbray, who provided the land for the building of Byland Abbey. Its treasures, built up from a succession of families, were dispersed by William Randolph Hearst, the American newspaper owner, who acquired them and moved many of the contents to a castle he owned in Wales. Since 1929 the castle has been used as a preparatory school for Ampleforth, the Roman Catholic public school. It has an original Norman keep with additions from the sixteenth and eighteenth centuries.

Clifford's Tower, York

Helmsley Castle, Helmsley, York.

The bustling market town of Helmsley is overlooked by the imposing ruins of Helmsley Castle, which was built between 1186 and 1227. Its keep, tower, curtain walls and domestic buildings provide an indication of the former strength of this fortress. To protect the gatehouse, a barbican was built with holes through which longbowmen could fire their arrows.

Probably because of its impregnability, the castle had to face few military onslaughts. Its most important test was in 1644, when for three months it held out against Sir Thomas Fairfax, the Parliamentary general. It was dismantled after its final surrender.

Knaresborough Castle, Knaresborough, North Yorkshire.

The castle ruins at Knaresborough overlook a deep gorge along which the river Nidd flows through the town. The castle was originally built in the eleventh century by a Norman nobleman but one of its most famous occupants was Queen Philippa, wife of Edward III, who pleaded for the lives of the burghers of Calais in 1347. It came to a gruesome end in 1646, when, as a Royalist garrison, its occupants were starved into submission by Parliamentary troops and the building was largely destroyed.

The ruins now seen date from the fourteenth century and consist mainly of the battered keep, which has a room filled with treasures; visitors may also see the dungeon. The castle courtyard is now laid out as a garden.

Middleham Castle, Middleham, Leyburn, North Yorkshire.

Middleham Castle earned the title of the Windsor of the North, so frequent were the visits of medieval monarchs and noblemen. It was owned by Richard Neville, Earl of Warwick, but is perhaps most famous for its associations with Richard III. As Duke of Gloucester, he was made Lord of the North by his elder brother, Edward IV, with control of England north of the Trent. During this period Richard lived at Middleham, his favourite

Middleham Castle.

castle, which he had obtained through marriage to one of the Neville family. His only son, also called Edward, was born and died there.

In its heyday Middleham Castle was one of the strongest fortresses in the north but towards the end of the fifteenth century it became untenanted and some of its stonework was used as material for other buildings in the area. The ruins of the castle stand on a high slope overlooking the river Ure and the top of the keep, which was one of the largest in England, is a magnificent vantage point from which to view the surrounding landscape.

Pickering Castle, Pickering, North Yorkshire.

Pickering gives its name to the vale between York and Scarborough. In the well preserved ruins of the castle on the north side of the town can be traced the form of the motte and bailey type of Norman structure. The motte remains but the original wooden defences were replaced with a stone keep in the twelfth century. The castle was in the possession of Thomas, Earl of Lancaster, a cousin of Edward II, of whom he was an active opponent. An earlier visitor was Henry II, who, while staying here, granted York its charter. The main part of the remains originates from the late eleventh and early twelfth centuries and the curtain walls and towers date mainly from the fourteenth century, when the castle was extended.

Richmond Castle, Richmond, North Yorkshire.

Early examples of Norman stonework can be seen at the triangular Richmond Castle in the east and west curtain walls and part of the gatehouse. Richmond also has an outstanding example of another feature of Norman castles, the keep, which here towers 100 feet (30 m) high, with walls 11 feet (3.4 m) thick, and affords the visitor one of the finest views in a county renowned for its breathtaking landscape.

Ripley Castle, Ripley, Harrogate, North Yorkshire.

Less strident than some of North Yorkshire's other castles but certainly no less picturesque is Ripley Castle. The quiet little village of Ripley is situated at a junction where the roads from Knaresborough, Harrogate and Ripon meet. The castle is almost hidden by trees in an area of flat land.

This castle has been in the ownership of the Ingilby family since 1350 and has figured hardly at all in great historic events. There was, however, one notable exception, when Oliver Cromwell sought refuge there after the Battle of Marston Moor, in which the then owner, Sir William Ingilby, had fought on the Royalist side. Cromwell got a frosty and inhospitable reception from Sir William's wife, who merely allowed him to rest on a settee and kept watch over him all night with two pistols on a table.

The castle is still a private house but is open to the public.

Scarborough Castle, Scarborough, North Yorkshire.

Scarborough Castle, dating from the twelfth century, was twice besieged and occupied by Parliamentarian forces, in 1643 and 1648, and the Quaker George Fox was imprisoned there in 1665. It was damaged by shell fire during the First World War. The ruins stand high on the Castle Rock headland, dominating Scarborough's two bays. The remains of the Roman signal station, one of a chain built between the Tees and the Humber to strengthen coastal defences in the fourth century, are to be seen on the edge of the cliff.

Skipton Castle, Skipton, North Yorkshire.

Skipton is an agricultural market town at 'the gateway to the Dales' and just inside the borders of North Yorkshire. The castle, alongside the church, stands prominently at the top of the High Street. The first castle here was built in the eleventh century and in the fourteenth it was acquired by the Clifford family, who rebuilt it in its present form, in which some Norman work remains. After a three year siege against Parliamentary forces in the Civil War, buildings were de-roofed but the castle was restored by Lady Anne Clifford, Countess of Pembroke. Part of the restored castle is built around the picturesque Conduit Court, in the centre of which stands a yew tree reputed to be more than three hundred years old. During the Second World War pictures and manuscripts from the British Museum were stored for safety in the Great Hall.

Spofforth Castle, Spofforth, Harrogate, North Yorkshire.

Spofforth is situated between Wetherby and Harrogate. Its now ruined castle is reputed to have been the birthplace of the rebellious Harry Hotspur (Henry Percy), whom Henry IV defeated and killed in 1403. It is an early fourteenth-century structure and the remains include a hall and a solar wing; the natural rock forms one of the ground-floor walls.

Bolton Abbey.

5
Monastic ruins

The abbeys and priories of Yorkshire exceed those of any other county in both numbers and magnificence. Many are situated in North Yorkshire, in settings that are outstandingly picturesque, so that a visit can be a memorable and moving experience. The peace and tranquility of these surroundings has to be experienced to be appreciated. In many cases the ruins are extensive and have been well preserved, often through the guardianship of the Historic Buildings and Monuments Commission. They are not only pleasantly placed to visit but an important record of building styles and architectural ornamentation from the past.

Bolton Abbey, Skipton, North Yorkshire. 4 miles (6 km) east of Skipton, just north of A59.

The ruins of Bolton Abbey — or, correctly, Bolton Priory — are set in spectacular surroundings: beautiful parkland with the gracefully curving river Wharfe and Bolton Hall, Yorkshire home of the Duke of Devonshire, nearby. The hall was built, as was often the practice, largely from the ruins of the old priory and incorporates its gateway. The hall is not open to the public.

The priory was established in 1154 and the ruins bear traces of several styles of architecture. It surrendered to officials of Henry VIII in 1538. The nave of the church escaped the destruction and dereliction of the other buildings after the Dissolution and has been used as the local parish church.

The priory was built on the site of a Saxon manor by Augustinian canons, who had earlier established themselves some miles away at Embsay, near Skipton. The canons built and extended the priory at a leisurely pace, extending over four hundred years, since it was still incomplete at the Dissolution. But in that time the canons had established themselves as one of the richest religious houses, much of their wealth being derived from the sale of wool from the huge flocks of sheep they grazed on the surrounding fells and the estates they owned.

The ruins are extensive and include a cloister, frater, chapter house, prior's lodging and the church.

There are extensive woodland and riverside walks and a nature trail. Nearby on the roadside is the elaborate Cavendish Pavilion, an ornate drinking fountain erected as a memorial to Lord Frederick Cavendish, who was murdered in Phoenix Park, Dublin, on 6th May 1882, only hours after his arrival as Chief Secretary for Ireland in Gladstone's government. 2 miles (3 km) away are the ruins of Barden Tower (see chapter 4).

Byland Abbey, Wass, York. 8 miles (13 km) west of Thirsk.

Not far from Coxwold, in the village of Wass, are the ruins of Byland Abbey, which was once the largest Cistercian church in Britain, more than 328 feet (100 m) long and 135 feet (41 m) wide across the transepts. It was founded in 1177 by monks from Furness Abbey in Cumbria and was their second choice of a site. They had earlier settled across the river Rye at what is now Old Byland but could not tolerate the confusion caused by the tolling of the bell at nearby Rievaulx Abbey. They moved on to the present site after four years of campanological confusion.

Edward II left stores and treasures at the abbey as he retreated from his ill-fated attempt to invade the Scots. His pursuers from across the border caused much damage when they ransacked the abbey in their pursuit of the English king.

The remains include the west front of the church, and the layout of the entire monastery, which had extensive cloisters, can be traced. Among the ruins of the west wall is a large rose window which, at 26 feet (8 m) in diameter, was one of the largest circular windows, and colourful medieval green and yellow tiles arranged in geometrical patterns can still be seen. A small museum on the site contains examples of the superb carving of the nave capitals.

Coverham Abbey, Coverham, Leyburn, North Yorkshire. 1½ miles (2.4 km) from Middleham.

Like Easby Abbey, Coverham was a house of the Premonstratensian canons, founded originally near Thirsk but transferred here about 1202. It was partly destroyed by Scots in the fourteenth century and later rebuilt. Rebellious monks in the Pilgrimage of Grace, a protest against the closure of religious houses, assembled at the abbey, but it was suppressed in 1536, by which time it had only an abbot and sixteen monks. There are now few remains and these are mainly of the monastic church. The site is in private grounds and permission has to be obtained to visit the remains.

Easby Abbey, Easby, Richmond, North Yorkshire. 1 mile (1.6 km) from Richmond.

The ruins of Easby Abbey are in a delightful setting on the banks of the river Swale, along which there is a picturesque walk from Richmond. A Premonstratensian abbey, Easby was founded in 1155 and dedicated to St Agatha. The ruins of the monastic buildings are considerable and include parts of the refectory and infirmary and a separate gatehouse, dating from the early thirteenth century. There also remain sections of the lower walls of the church, woodwork from which has been used in St Mary's church at Richmond and at Wensley.

Fountains Abbey, Ripon, Yorkshire. 4 miles (6 km) west of Ripon.

From unpropitious beginnings Fountains Abbey became the richest and most powerful Cistercian monastery in England. Its remains are claimed to be the finest monastic ruin in western Europe.

Its foundation in 1132 was the result of a secession by a group of thirteen monks from the Benedictine York Abbey who sought a stricter way of life. At the start it was a life of considerable deprivation. The first buildings were destroyed in a fire started maliciously by enemies of the abbot. Their reconstruction took thirty years from 1148 to 1179. Today, the setting of the monastic ruins is tranquil and picturesque but the monks who selected the site found, according to contemporary accounts, a place of thorn and rocks — 'a better dwelling for wild beasts than for men'.

Most of the ruined buildings date from the twelfth century but the Chapel of the Nine Altars at the east end of the church was built between 1203 and 1247 and the northern bell tower was added at the end of the fifteenth century. After the initial hardships, the monks became pioneer developers of the wool and lead trades and came to possess vast areas of land stretching as far as Penyghent high in the Pennines.

After the Dissolution, when the abbot was hanged, the abbey passed into private ownership. Glass and lead from the roofs were taken away and the infirmary was demolished to provide stone for the building of Fountains Hall nearby (see Chapter 7).

The sheer delight of the surroundings is complemented by the adjoining grounds and lakes of Studley Royal Park, with its 650 acres (263 ha) of woodland, park and ornamental gardens. The lakes and gardens were landscaped in the eighteenth century. Studley Hall was destroyed in a fire in 1946.

Jervaulx Abbey, Ripon, North Yorkshire. On A6108 between Masham and Middleham.

Monks from Jervaulx Abbey were among the originators of horse breeding in the area. They bred their own horses to transport them to their estates in the remote dales. It is the breeding of racehorses that is now a major industry in the area. Another industry for which the monks were responsible was the manufacture, from ewes' milk, of the famous Wensleydale cheese.

The monks had been offered land near Askrigg in 1144 but this site proved too bleak and they moved to the site of the present ruins in 1156. Like their Cistercian colleagues at Fountains Abbey, the monks of Jervaulx also became substantial landowners, eventually owning most of Wensleydale. But it all ended

Easby Abbey gatehouse.

Fountains Abbey.

ignominiously when the last abbot, Adam Sedbergh, was hanged as one of the leaders of the Pilgrimage of Grace, the ill-fated protest against the closure of religious houses. Two years later came the Dissolution of the Monasteries and the destruction of Jervaulx along with the rest. Much of the stone was pilfered by local builders. The church and the chapter house disappeared but from the remains of the domestic buildings the ground plan of the monastery can be discerned.

Kirkham Abbey, York. 12 miles (19 km) north-east of York.

Kirkham, like most ruined monasteries, is located beside a river, in this case the Derwent. A house of Augustinian canons, it was founded in 1125.

The main attraction to present-day visitors, apart from the beautiful and peaceful surroundings, is the thirteenth-century gatehouse, which still has magnificent sculpture and carvings, particularly a series of shields bearing coats of arms which are important examples of early heraldic art. The remaining stones set in the turf present an indication of the ground plan of the abbey and in the ruined cloister, in the former lavatorium, there is traceried panelling dated 1300.

Mount Grace Priory, Northallerton, North Yorkshire. 7 miles (11 km) north-east of Northallerton.

Thomas Holland, Duke of Surrey, was the founder of Mount Grace Priory in 1398. It is regarded as the finest example in Britain of a charterhouse or Carthusian monastery. At its foundation it accommodated twenty monks, who conformed to a strict, hermit-like routine, living in separate cells and working alone and in silence in a garden adjoining each cell. Their food was passed to them through a hatch, shaped and constructed so that the server was neither seen nor touched by the monk. They met only in the church for matins, vespers and services on feast days. Part of the priory was made into a private house after the Dissolution.

The ruins include the outer court and gatehouse, guest houses and barns, the church and the cloister, with the remains of the cells in which the monks lived their isolated lives. One of these has been restored to its original condition.

Rievaulx Abbey, Helmsley, York. 3 miles (5 km) north-west of Helmsley.

Cistercian monks from Clairvaux in France started building Rievaulx, their first monastery in Britain, in about 1132. The main buildings were completed in the twelfth century, by the end of which the abbey had 140 monks and five hundred lay brothers. Enlargements were made in the thirteenth century. By the time of the Dissolution, however, most of the lay brothers had fled and there were left a mere handful of monks. The monks of Rievaulx, like those of other great abbeys in Yorkshire, were sheep farmers on a large scale and gained much wealth from this source.

One of the abbey's chief attractions is its picturesque setting in a narrow, tree-lined valley of the river Rye. Its beauty and serenity have been portrayed by many famous artists.

The remains of the monastic buildings extend over a considerable area and have been well preserved. The nave, which dates from 1135-40, is the earliest large Cistercian nave in Britain and is older than any remaining in France, from where the Rievaulx monks originated. The choir, one of the finest examples of its period, was part of the thirteenth-century enlargements.

A breathtaking view of the abbey remains can be seen from the heights of the Rievaulx Terrace, which overlooks the ruins.

The eighteenth-century Tuscan temple at the southern end of the Terrace has been restored by the National Trust.

Whitby Abbey, Whitby, North Yorkshire.

The spectacular abbey ruins standing on the high east cliff at Whitby are a landmark for mariners and were damaged by enemy shelling in the First World War. An early Saxon monastery was founded here in AD 657 with St Hilda, a Northumbrian princess, as abbess. The monastery was destroyed by Vikings in 870 but was refounded as a Benedictine abbey at the end of the eleventh century. It was the venue for the Synod in 664 at which the supremacy of Rome over the Celtic church was established. The monastery produced two notable figures of early history: Caedmon, the first English poet, and St John of Beverley, whose shrine is in Beverley Minster.

Excavations have disclosed evidence of the monastery's origins, including some of the small cells occupied by the monks. Remains of the refounded monastery are alongside the main ruins, which are of the thirteenth-century church, two of the main facades of which are still standing.

Rievaulx Abbey.

6
Cathedrals, churches and chapels

Arkengarthdale: St Mary the Virgin. In addition to Robert Thompson's woodwork, there are examples of Dent marble in two large memorial tablets on either side of the sanctuary.

Askrigg, Wensleydale: St Oswald. This is a fine example of a late Perpendicular church. The nave ceiling has huge moulded beams of the sixteenth century and the tower from the fifteenth. The church contains many memorials to the Metcalfes, a notable Wensleydale family.

Aysgarth, Wensleydale: St Andrew. The church, a mile (1.6 km) from the village near the river, underwent major restoration in Victorian times but still has a magnificent screen brought from Jervaulx Abbey after the Dissolution, and pews bearing poppy heads, the work of the outstanding Ripon carvers. The oldest part of the church is its tower. The churchyard extends to 5 acres (2 ha).

Bedale, Wensleydale: St Gregory. A wall painting and Dutch panelling are among the features of interest in this church, the nave of which dates to the thirteenth century. The tower was probably used as a watchtower during Scottish raids in the fourteenth century. The largest of the church bells is over four hundred years old and came from the ruined Jervaulx Abbey.

Beverley Minster. It took nearly two hundred years before Beverley Minster, built on an ancient religious site, was completed in 1400: it thus incorporates a variety of styles of ecclesiastical architecture. The 163 foot (50 m) high towers are supported by elaborate buttresses and have fourteen ornamental pinnacles piercing the sky. The west front is considered to be one of the finest examples of Gothic architecture in Europe. Inside is a thousand-year-old fridstool which afforded sanctuary for fugitives, and also notable is the Percy Shrine, the richly carved canopy of which has been described as the finest piece of work of the finest craftsmen of the finest period in British building. There are also some beautifully carved misericords.

Beverley: St Mary. A near rival to the Minster for the splendour of its architecture, St Mary's was founded in the twelfth century to serve the guilds and freemen of the town. This is reflected by the Minstrel's Pillar, constructed by the Guild of Minstrels, on which are depicted in the original colours five minstrels and their instruments. The wooden ceilings and carvings are also of interest. Lewis Carroll attended St Mary's while staying with friends and it is reputed that one of the carved animals guarding a chapel doorway, a hare carrying a satchel over its shoulder, was his inspiration for the March Hare in *Alice in Wonderland*.

Bridlington: Priory Church. This is another ecclesiastical treasure. Over four centuries Bridlington Priory became one of the richest foundations until it was sacked at the time of the Dissolution. The nave was left because it served as the parish church. Restoration took place over thirty years from 1850 under the direction of Sir Gilbert Scott and resulted in the present splendid building with its high hammerbeam roof.

Burnsall, Wharfedale: St Wilfred. An earlier church was rebuilt in the sixteenth century, when the tower was added, and there were restorations in 1612 and 1859. There is an early Norman font and the church contains gravestones of the Viking period. In the north chapel is an alabaster carving of the Adoration of the Magi dating from the thirteenth century. The village stocks are preserved in the churchyard, where there is also a modern monument by the sculptor Eric Gill to the Dawson family.

Clapham, West Craven: St James. The tower is of fourteenth-century date, but the present church was rebuilt in 1814 and underwent restorations in 1899 and 1903. It contains several wall tablets and other memorials to members of the Farrer family, who lived nearby at Ingleborough Hall.

Coverham, Coverdale: Holy Trinity. The church dates from about 1250 and the tower is of the fifteenth century. The present building was restored by the Victorians in 1854 and 1878. Over the south doorway is a lintel stone of pre-Conquest times. The church is now closed.

Easby, Swaledale: St Agatha. Originally an aisleless Norman building, the church was rebuilt in the Perpendicular period. The chancel contains thirteenth-century terracotta frescoes and there are fragments elsewhere in the church. The paintings show biblical scenes or portray agricultural workers in different seasons. The church has an ornate Norman font and the upper part of a two-storey porch was formerly the priest's room.

Giggleswick, Ribblesdale: St Alkelda. This large Perpendicular church until 1838 served as parish church for the adjoining town of Settle. Parts of the present building date from 1400. It has some fine seventeenth-century woodwork, including the pulpit, which has the names and badges of the twelve tribes of Israel carved on it. It was within the church that the public school of Giggleswick, founded by James Carr, had its origins.

Hedon, Humberside. Hedon church is one of the large Holderness churches that could well be mistaken for a cathedral, so splendid and glorious is its size and appearance. It is known as the 'King' of Holderness: the church at Patrington is the 'Queen'.

Horton-in-Ribblesdale: St Oswald. A Norman church, dated about 1100, with restorations in 1400 and in Victorian times, it has a Perpendicular tower, porch and windows. There is a large decorated Norman font. A fragment of stained glass in one of its windows is believed to portray the head of Thomas à Becket.

Hubberholme, Wharfedale: St Michael and All Angels. The tower arch and south doorway are of the Transitional period but the church was restored in 1863. Of particular interest is the rare rood loft on which the arms of the Percy family and the date of 1558 are carved. The pews are the work of Robert Thompson.

Kirby Malham, Malhamdale: St Michael the Archangel. This large church is an outstanding example of a Perpendicular church with a spacious and interesting interior. The font, of Danish origin, was found among rubbish in the churchyard in the nineteenth century and restored to its place in the church. Two entries in the parish register of 1655 are signed by Oliver Cromwell as a witness to marriages and a framed copy is in the vestry.

Lastingham: The church here was built on one of Britain's oldest sacred sites. Most of the church was built in 1078 and in Norman times it was a small priory. The only light in the building comes from a small window at one end.

Linton-in-Craven: St Michael and All Angels. Dating from about 1150, the church was enlarged and almost rebuilt in the Decorated period in the sixteenth century and underwent Victorian restoration. A rare crucifix of the ninth and tenth centuries hangs on a pillar of the south arcade.

Beverley Minster.

Ripon Cathedral.

Middleham, Wensleydale: St Mary and St Alkelda. The present church, restored in 1878, dates from 1280, although there was an earlier church on the site. It has associations with Richard, Duke of Gloucester (later Richard III). Charles Kingsley, the author, was at one time a titular canon of the church.

Patrington, Humberside. Many superlatives have been used to describe this elegant fourteenth-century parish church, which, looking more like a cathedral, has been titled 'Queen of Holderness'. Experts place it among the finest dozen churches in Britain: Sir Nikolaus Pevsner said that for sheer architectural beauty few parish churches in England can compare.

Pickering: St Peter and St Paul. The tall fourteenth-century spire of the church provides a landmark. There are well preserved Norman arches but the most notable feature of the church is the colourful fifteenth-century murals depicting biblical scenes and the lives of the saints. These are among the finest in Britain.

Richmond, Swaledale: St Mary. The tower, built in 1400, has been retained but the church was largely restored in 1860 by Sir Gilbert Scott, who kept two of the Norman pillars. The carved choir stalls are reputed to have come from Easby Abbey.

Ripon Cathedral. The founding of a monastery in AD 650 started the growth around it of the town of Ripon. St Wilfrid, who became abbot in 671, was an arbiter between Celtic and Roman expressions of the Christian faith in Saxon England and is still commemorated annually with a festival in the town.

Wilfrid's church was one of the finest stone buildings in northern Europe. The most historic part of the present building is the Saxon crypt, which survived the destruction of Wilfrid's church by Viking pirates. It is the oldest part of any British cathedral and is open to inspection.

The cathedral has a mixture of styles — transitional Norman, Early English and Perpendicular. In the fifteenth century it was partly transformed into a Perpendicular church but the builders did not complete the work. This gives it another unique feature: at the crossing the tower has two pointed arches where the transformation was begun and two round ones from the earlier church. The west front is Early English, with lancet windows a particular feature, and presents an elegant sight when the cathedral is approached from the town along a narrow shopping street.

The nave, 133 feet (41 m) long and 87 feet (27 m) wide, is the fifth largest in Britain. Immediately above the high altar, the east window has some fine tracery and there is a screen dated 1494.

The cathedral's fine ceilings have been restored to their former glory and the reredos, by Sir Gilbert Scott, commemorates victims of the First World War.

Another feature of the cathedral is its intricate wood carving, in particular misericords beneath the fifteenth-century choir stalls which depict a variety of biblical scenes.

The present building became a cathedral in 1836.

Selby Abbey. Selby Abbey was founded in 1069 with the approval of William I but all the buildings except the church were pulled down after the Dissolution and the nave of the abbey church became the parish church in 1618, which it remains. The south and west parts of the nave are Norman, the east Early English and the middle of the Transitional period.

Its building by Benedictine monks in 1069 was earlier than the other Benedictine abbeys in the North. The central tower collapsed in 1690 and several fires have taken their toll of the original building. It is, however, one of the few remaining abbey churches to have survived and still be in use in Britain.

The church is 300 feet (91 m) long and has four double bays. Sir Gilbert Scott was responsible for restorations in 1871-3 and Oldred Scott rebuilt the crossing tower in 1908, two years after a disastrous fire had damaged the entire fabric. The fire also badly damaged ceiling bosses but some of these, showing animals, birds, fishes, flowers and angels, were rescued and reinstated.

The church has some fine tracery, stone panelling and arcading, and a number of modern statues. There is a plain Norman font with a cover made by fifteenth-century craftsmen.

Of the stained glass, the Jesse window at the east end is of particular interest. It contains sixty-eight small figures and although restored dates from about 1330. There are also medieval pieces in other windows in the chancel and sacristy.

The Latham Chapel, founded in 1476 by John Latham, Archbishop of York and later of Canterbury, is on the east side of the church.

Those with an interest in music should try to visit the church while it is in use, for it possesses one of the finest church organs in Britain.

Skipton, Airedale. The parish church overlooks the busy main street. It was built in the reign of Richard III and contains many monuments and tombs of the Clifford family who lived at the neighbouring Skipton Castle. One of the tombs now forms the altar.

Wensley, Wensleydale: Holy Trinity. The church was built in various styles from Norman times. The west tower was rebuilt in 1719. The main attractions of the church are in its interior — rich furnishings, including a carved screen from Easby Abbey, finely carved choir stalls, and some of the finest medieval brasses in the north of England.

Whitby: St Mary. Reached by climbing 199 steps, the church has strong links with fishermen. The interior has beautiful Georgian woodwork, reputedly fitted by ships' carpenters.

York Minster. Of all the splendid religious buildings of North Yorkshire and North Humberside, York Minster stands supreme — the largest Gothic church in England, its three towers dominating the city and beyond. The present building is the fifth church to be built on the site. It took two and a half centuries to complete — it was finished in 1480 — and incorporates Early English, Decorated and Perpendicular styles.

It has many outstanding features, including a richly sculptured fifteenth-century stone choir screen, but its greatest glory is in its stained glass windows, of which there are over a hundred, containing glass from the twelfth to the twentieth centuries. The great East Window, dating from 1408, is one of the largest in the world; at the western end of the nave is another huge window, dating from 1338, its tracery in the form of a heart; in the north transept are thirteenth-century lancet windows known as the 'Five Sisters'; and in the south transept a rose window combining the white rose of York and the red rose of Lancaster.

In 1967 serious structural damage was discovered in the minster, caused by inadequate foundations, particularly of the huge central tower. In the ensuing restoration thousands of tons of concrete were poured in to underpin the foundations.

The costly restoration had its advantages: it demonstrated examples of modern craftsmanship to compare with those centuries old and also led to the discovery of new treasures, many of which are now displayed in a museum in the undercroft.

Robert Thompson. In many other churches, large and small, there are also examples of modern craftsmanship alongside the historic masterpieces. An instance is the work of Robert Thompson, a carpenter from Kilburn, who became identified as the 'Mouse Man' because he always carved a mouse as his trade mark on any item he produced. Much of Thompson's craftsmanship can be seen in churches in North Yorkshire: he produced pews and other woodwork in St John's, Appletreewick, a reredos and altar table for St Mary's, Arkengarthdale, pews at St Michael's, Hubberholme, the lectern, prayer desk and pulpit in St Matthew's, Leyburn, the pulpit at St John's, East Witton, and much woodwork at St Mary's, Richmond, to list only a few examples.

The Anglican church has the monopoly of ancient buildings but there are other religious buildings still in use that are of considerable interest. George Fox, founder of the Society of Friends, had great influence in the Dales as he travelled the country, making conversions to the Quaker faith.

Airton. Not far from Skipton, in the village of Airton, a meeting house was built in 1700 with a secluded burial ground behind. It was built opposite their house by William and Alice Ellis, two early converts to the faith, who travelled to America on preaching missions.

Countersett. Above Semerwater, near Bainbridge in Wensleydale, is the small village of Countersett, where a meeting house which was built in 1710 is still used from time to time. At the southern end of Semerwater one of the elders, John Fothergill, lived at Carr End. He, too, visited America and his son, Dr John Fothergill, who became a notable physician in London, was founder of Ackworth School, a Quaker establishment near Pontefract.

Settle. The Friends' meeting house was built at Settle in 1678. At that time, like many other Quaker meeting houses, it was only a shell-like building, but later the roof was raised architecturally to fit in a gallery. It was built on a plot of land, a former pig yard, which the Friends had rented and used as a burial ground.

Skipton. A meeting house in Skipton was built in 1693, along a beckside alleyway which was later named Quaker Place. The building was for some years used as both meeting room and schoolroom and in the 1760s dividing screens were added that could separate women's meetings from those of the men or be lifted to provide a large meeting room when necessary.

Winterburn. Parts of the Yorkshire Dales were early centres of nonconformity. One of these was Winterburn, near Gargrave, where a Congregational church, built in 1704, was in use by followers of that denomination until 1880. The building was reopened two years later and has since then been a chapel of ease to Gargrave church.

York. The oldest dissenting chapel in York, the Unitarian Chapel in St Saviourgate, was built by Congregationalists in 1693. It was built in the shape of a Greek cross, with a central tower at the intersection. Pews and communion rail date from about 1860 but the pulpit is believed to be original late seventeenth-century and there are wall tablets by noted local masons.

In 1839-40 York Methodists built their Centenary Chapel, also in St Saviourgate. This building has an elegant facade with an Ionic portico, but the rest of the building is in brick. The interior is thought by many people to be superior to the exterior. It has an ornate ceiling and nine pillars with gilt Corinthian capitals support the gallery. Magnificent Spanish mahogany was used for much of the woodwork, including the pulpit and organ.

York Minster.

ABOVE: *The Orangery at Burton Agnes Hall.*
BELOW: *The laundry at Beningbrough Hall.*

7
Historic houses and gardens

The great houses of North Yorkshire and North Humberside vary in period and style from Norman to Victorian Gothic. Examples of craftsmanship of high quality are to be found within the buildings. Fortunately for the modern visitor, not only have the buildings been preserved but much is still in evidence of their original contents, often in the surroundings where the items have lain for centuries.

The designers of the houses and their contents were often local men who made their reputations in Yorkshire and went on to achieve distinction elsewhere — men like John Carr, the York architect, much of whose work is to be seen in the area, Sir John Vanbrugh, whose stately design for Castle Howard was his first adventure into architecture, and Robert Adam and Thomas Chippendale, whose masterly work is frequently evident.

Beningbrough Hall, York. Telephone: York (0904) 470715. 8 miles (13 km) north-west of York. *National Trust.*

Surrounded by a beautiful wooded park near the river Ouse, south-facing Beningbrough Hall was built about 1716 for John Bourchier, probably by Thomas Archer and under the supervision of William Thornton, a carpenter-architect of York, whose influence is seen in the intricate carving of the oak staircase with its parqueted treads. The tall entrance hall rises through two floors. Work of other craftsmen from nearby York is apparent in the carved friezes in the drawing room, saloon and state bedroom.

A hundred portraits from the National Portrait Gallery, hung in the main rooms, form a national collection of portraits of notable personalities of the period 1688-1760 by, among others, Sir Godfrey Kneller, Gainsborough and Reynolds, illustrating the theme 'The Country House and the Portrait'. Complementing this collection are exhibits depicting domestic life of the same period. Of particular interest is the Victorian laundry.

The Bourchier family line died out in 1827 and the Dawnay family became owners. The hall became the home of the tenth Earl of Chesterfield in 1917. The Treasury accepted the hall and park in part payment of death duties and it passed to the National Trust when the countess died in 1957. It was reopened in 1979 after a major restoration.

Burton Agnes Hall, Burton Agnes, Driffield, North Humberside. Telephone: Burton Agnes (026 289) 324. 5½ miles (9 km) south-west of Bridlington.

A fine example of late Elizabethan architecture, with the royal arms carved over the front entrance, the present hall dates from 1600 with an Inigo Jones addition of 1620, but evidence of its Norman predecessor survives in the courtyard. The entrance is through an ornately decorated porch and the house features a finely carved staircase, ceilings, and overmantels carved in wood, stone and plaster. The collection of old and modern paintings contains work by Cezanne, Corot, Gauguin and Renoir. The hall is still occupied by descendants of the family who originally built it.

Burton Constable Hall, Hull. Telephone: Skirlaugh (0401) 62400. 8 miles (13 km) east of Hull.

A 200 acre (81 ha) country park with many family attractions surrounds the hall, which is one of the finest of stately homes. Built originally in 1570, the mansion was remodelled in the Georgian period by the owner, William Constable, who spared no expense and employed the master designers of the period such as Robert Adam, James Wyatt and John Carr. Part of Constable's personal suite was the Blue Drawing Room, which contains vases reputed to have been bought from Napoleon's sister. The long gallery, which contains a fifteenth-century Flemish stained glass window, was the creation of Cuthbert Constable in 1736.

A Victorian member of the family, Sir Clifford Constable, was noted for the huge fetes he held in the grounds and for his early encouragement of brass bands by holding one of the first band contests there in 1845.

The grounds were landscaped by Lancelot (Capability) Brown and include 4 acres (1.6 ha) of lawns and gardens and extensive lakes, with adjacent picnic areas.

Carlton Towers, Carlton, Goole, North Humberside. Telephone: Goole (0405) 860243. 6 miles (10 km) south of Selby.

Built on land owned by the Duke of Norfolk's ancestors since the Norman Conquest, Carlton Towers, the Duke's Yorkshire home, is the most complete Victorian Gothic house still in use as a family home. Its seventeenth-century origins — it was built in 1614 — were skilfully disguised in a major remodelling of the house by Pugin from 1871 to 1877. There are exquisite examples of Victorian craftsmanship, carved woodwork, stained glass and metalwork, particularly in the state rooms, which J. F. Bentley, the architect of Westminster Cathedral, remodelled. The house contains a priest's hiding hole and there are paintings from the collection of Prince Henry Benedict, Cardinal York, the last of the Stuarts, and an exhibition of family costumes and uniforms.

Castle Howard, York. Telephone: Coneysthorpe (065 384) 333. 6 miles (10 km) west of Malton.

Charles Howard, third Earl of Carlisle, originally commissioned Talman, who had worked at Chatsworth House, to build Castle Howard on the site of a former castle, but they quarrelled over payment. Howard then invited Sir John Vanbrugh to submit designs. It was Vanbrugh's first building design and, besides his success as a dramatist, he went on to become one of the finest of eighteenth-century architects. At Castle Howard, built between 1699 and 1726, he worked closely with Nicholas Hawksmoor and designed the first private house with a dome, which, with the decoration of beautiful frescoes, dominates the main hall. A fire in 1940 destroyed the original but it was immediately replaced and the painted ceilings were recreated in 1962-3 by Scott Nedd, a Canadian artist. Hawksmoor was the designer of the magnificent mausoleum.

Horace Walpole in 1772 wrote of the splendours of the place: 'Nobody had told me that I should see a place, a town, a fortified city, temples on high places, woods worthy of being each a metropolis of the Druids, the noblest lawn in the world fenced by half the horizon and a mausoleum that would tempt me to be buried alive; in short, I have seen gigantic places before but never a sublime one.'

The whole interior is rich with treasures from all over the world. On the grand staircase are the Soho tapestries of John Vanderbank, specially woven for the house in 1714. The long gallery contains a magnificent collection of paintings by Holbein, Van Dyck, Kneller, Lawrence and others, and the house is furnished with equally magnificent examples of the work of Adam, Sheraton and Chippendale. In the chapel is the altar from the temple of Delphi which Nelson saved from the French at Naples and gave to Lady Hamilton's husband, who, in turn, gave it to the fifth Earl of Carlisle.

The fireplace surrounds in the hall are easily mistaken for marble but they are made from a mixture of plaster and marble chippings, a method known as scagliola, the use of which at Castle Howard is believed to be earliest in Britain.

In the Stable Court are the Costume Galleries containing fashions from the eighteenth to the twentieth centuries (see chapter 8).

Burton Constable Hall.

Castle Howard.

Constable Burton Hall, Leyburn, North Yorkshire. Telephone: Bedale (0677) 50428. 3 miles (5 km) from Leyburn.

The hall, at the gateway to Wensleydale, was designed by the famous Yorkshire architect John Carr and completed in 1768. It is not open to the public but the beautiful gardens and grounds are. They contain a splendid display in season of daffodils, an interesting collection of alpines and extensive borders of roses and shrubs. In the park is a small lake inhabited by wildfowl.

Ebberston Hall, Ebberston, Scarborough, North Yorkshire. 11 miles (18 km) south-west of Scarborough on the main Pickering road.

Colin Campbell, the distinguished Scottish-born architect who later became architect to the Prince of Wales and surveyor of works at Greenwich Hospital, designed Ebberston Hall in 1718 for William Thompson, a Member of Parliament. Its chief feature was a magnificent water garden with a long canal and cascade in the Italian style but nothing can now be seen of that except a few remains. Architecturally the hall is often described as a Palladian villa but the late Sir Nikolaus Pevsner wrote that Ebberston was no more than a summer pavilion of three bays and far too animated and varied to be seriously Palladian.

It has a large doorway with Tuscan columns and, internally, a simple plan with elaborately decorated rooms on either side of a short corridor which runs from the doorway to a loggia at the back with more Tuscan columns Inside there are Ionic and Corinthian pilasters and rich friezes. Its elaborate woodwork and cornices have been compared with those at Castle Howard and Beningbrough Hall.

Fountains Hall, Ripon, North Yorkshire. Telephone: Sawley (076 586) 639. 2 miles (3 km) west of Ripon. *National Trust.*

A beautiful stone-built Jacobean house adjoining the majestic ruins of Fountains Abbey, Fountains Hall was built about 1611, largely with stone from the ruins, and there is in the chapel room a stone fireplace also taken from the old abbey. The hall contains a collection of early eighteenth-century pewter plate, fine tapestries and period furniture.

Built on the side of a valley, the house is unusually high, reaching five storeys, but is not very deep. The main architectural features are at the entrance front, with its recessed bays; above the entrance, and further recessed, is a semicircular window which, with other large windows on either side, illuminates the great chamber.

Markenfield Hall, Ripon, North Yorkshire. 3 miles (5 km) south of Ripon on A61 road.

This fourteenth-century building is a fine example of a fortified English manor house. It has fifteenth- and sixteenth-century additions to the buildings, which are surrounded by a water-filled moat. One of the most interesting features of the house is the banqueting hall, which still has some of its original windows. The kitchens, containing an enormous fireplace, are also interesting.

Newburgh Priory, Coxwold, York. Telephone: Coxwold (034 76) 435. 1 mile (1.6 km) from Coxwold.

Newburgh Priory was originally built by Augustinian monks in 1145 and additions were made in 1568 and 1720-60. It has been the home of one family and its descendants since 1538. The owner from 1647 to 1700 was Lord Fauconberg, who married Oliver Cromwell's daughter. It is claimed that the exhumed body of Cromwell was brought north and buried in a tomb here.

In the grounds is a beautiful water garden, well stocked with rare alpines, rhododendrons and other plants.

Newby Hall, Ripon, North Yorkshire. Telephone: Boroughbridge (090 12) 2583. 4 miles (6 km) south-east of Ripon.

The original hall, built about 1695, was redesigned by Robert Adam and is now regarded as one of his best houses. It contains a fine collection of sculpture and there are also Gobelin tapestries and Chippendale furniture. On the ceiling of the tapestry room are medallions, painted by Zucci, representing the four seasons, and the sculpture galleries, which Adam designed in the Roman style, comprise two rooms with a connecting rotunda.

The hall is surrounded by 25 acres (10 ha) of parkland and gardens sloping down to the banks of the river Ure and noted for the colourful seasonal displays of herbaceous plants. There are also rock gardens and waterfalls and many public amenities, including a picnic area.

Norton Conyers, Ripon, North Yorkshire. Telephone: Melmerby (076 584) 333. 3½ miles (6 km) north of Ripon.

Successive generations of the Graham family have occupied this fine Jacobean house for over 350 years. It was built in 1624 and stands in parkland. It has a large eighteenth-century walled garden from which plants and, in season, soft fruits are now sold.

The house contains a collection of family portraits and a display of Victorian dresses and children's costumes and toys. There are also items associated with Charlotte Brontë, who is reputed to have used the house as one of the models for Thornfield Hall, Rochester's residence in *Jane Eyre.*

Ebberston Hall.

Newby Hall.

Nunnington Hall, Nunnington, York. Telephone: Nunnington (043 95) 283. 4½ miles (7 km) south-east of Helmsley. *National Trust.*

A late seventeenth-century large manor house beside the river Rye and near a picturesque packhorse bridge, Nunnington Hall has a variety of architectural styles. It was tenanted in the mid sixteenth century by Dr Robert Huickes, who served as physician to Henry VIII, Catherine Parr, Edward VI and Elizabeth I. It fell to him to inform Elizabeth that she could never have children.

A subsequent owner was the first Viscount Preston, who married Lady Anne Howard, daughter of the Earl of Carlisle from nearby Castle Howard, and was Charles II's ambassador at the court of Louis XIV.

The house was later tenanted by farmers but became dilapidated until 1870, when it was repaired. There is a fine panelled hall and staircase and exhibits include tapestries and china and the Carlisle collection of miniature furnished rooms.

Rudding Park, Harrogate, North Yorkshire. Telephone: Harrogate (0423) 871350. 3 miles (5 km) from Harrogate.

Humphry Repton landscaped the beautiful parkland in which this nineteenth-century Regency country house is situated. The gardens are noted for the shrubberies and splendid rhododendron walk and there is much woodland with stately oak and beech trees. The house contains a collection of figurines, fine tapestries, porcelain and paintings.

Shandy Hall, Coxwold, York. Telephone: Coxwold (034 76) 465.

Shandy Hall was the home of the great English novelist Laurence Sterne, who was appointed vicar of Coxwold in 1760. He wrote much of *Tristram Shandy* and the whole of *A Sentimental Journey* here. The house has an interesting architectural history. It was built originally as a timber-framed open-hall house in the fifteenth century and was modernised in the seventeenth century; Sterne named it Shandy Hall and made further additions, including a Georgian facade at one end. It is a rambling house with rooms of curious shapes and sizes and has changed little since Sterne's occupancy, particularly the small book-lined study on the ground floor where he wrote his own famous books.

Sledmere House, Sledmere, Driffield, North Humberside. Telephone: Driffield (0377) 86208. 8 miles (13 km) north-west of Driffield.

This is a Georgian manor house built in 1751 and enlarged by the addition of a 100 foot (30 m) long library in 1787. The interior contains furniture by Chippendale and Sheraton and decorated plasterwork in the Adam style by Joseph Rose. One room is decorated with unusual Turkish tiles and there are paintings and porcelain on display. The surrounding gardens and parkland are another example of the work of Lancelot (Capability) Brown. The house has been the home of the Sykes family since it was first built.

Sutton Park, Sutton-on-the-Forest, York. Telephone: Easingwold (0347) 810249. 8 miles (13 km) north of York on B1363 road.

An early Georgian house, Sutton Park was built in 1730, with beautiful decorated plasterwork by Cortese and fine furniture by Chippendale and Sheraton and French craftsmen. There are paintings and porcelain among the contents, some of which were originally in Buckingham House, now Buckingham Palace, when it was the home of the Duke of Buckingham.

Capability Brown was responsible for the gardens, one of the features of which is a rose garden. There is a Georgian ice house in the grounds and there are many woodland walks and a nature trail.

Treasurer's House, Chapter House Street, York. Telephone: York (0904) 24247. *National Trust.*

One of York's heritage of fine and interesting buildings, the house stands on the site of a Roman building, the remains of the base of a pillar still being visible in the cellar. It was the home of the Treasurers of York Minster from William the Conqueror's time until the reign of Henry VIII, who did away with that office in 1547.

A succession of private owners made many alterations. The present house, which dates mainly from the seventeenth and eighteenth centuries, and nearby Grays Court were originally one building: they were divided in 1720. King Edward VII and Queen Alexandra, when Prince and Princess of Wales, stayed in the house during a visit to York in 1900 and the rooms they occupied are displayed.

There is a fine collection of period furniture given by the last private owner, Frank Green, when he handed over the house to the National Trust in 1950. In the basement an exhibition illustrates many of the personalities associated with the house.

GARDENS OPEN TO THE PUBLIC

Burnby Hall Gardens, Pocklington, York. Telephone: Pocklington (075 92) 2068 and 2114.

Visiting specialists from all over the world come to see the rare collection of water-lilies, for which these gardens are famous. There are fifty varieties, which provide a colourful spectacle in the main flowering season from July to early September and are regarded as the most outstanding collection of their kind in Europe.

The hall and gardens were bequeathed to the people of Pocklington in 1962 on the death of the owner, Major P. M. Stewart, who, with his wife, had travelled the world before settling down here to develop the gardens. The hall is now used as council offices and contains Major Stewart's interesting collection of sporting trophies in a small museum. The gardens, administered by a trust, are open, free to residents of the town and at a nominal charge to others. Major Stewart had two lakes, covering 2 acres (0.8 ha), built and stocked, mainly to satisfy his passion for trout fishing, but in the 1930s his interest in gardening prevailed and different species of water-lily were planted in specially built soil beds. The trees and shrubs include varieties from different parts of the world and there are interesting rock gardens near the smaller of the two lakes. There are altogether 8 acres (3 ha) of garden.

Duncombe Park, Helmsley, York. ½ mile (800 m) west of Helmsley.

The classical style house, the ancestral home of the Earls of Faversham, was designed locally but strongly influenced by the work of Vanbrugh, who built nearby Castle Howard. The large garden has eighteenth-century terraces with woodland walks and fine views of the Rye valley and there are also two temples of the same period.

Harlow Car Garden, Harrogate, North Yorkshire. Telephone: Harrogate (0423) 65418. 1½ miles (2.4 km) from Harrogate.

Set in beautiful surroundings are the 40 acres (16 ha) of trial grounds and ornamental gardens of the Northern Horticultural Society, where new plants are tested under severe northern conditions. In addition to the test areas, there are rock gardens, rose gardens and woodlands.

This is far from being a domain of the expert horticulturalist only. The staff welcomes beginners and first-time garden owners. The gardens are designed to have something of

HORSEDRAWN VEHICLES

interest to gardeners all the year round but especially in summer visitors are treated to a blaze of colour. Even native wild flowers have been introduced. There are also vegetable and fruit gardens and rare and unusual flowers, shrubs and trees. The whole area will either spur the amateur gardener on to better results or make him abandon his efforts in despair.

Parceval Hall Gardens, Appletreewick, Skipton, North Yorkshire. Telephone: Burnsall (075 672) 214. 2 miles (3 km) from Appletreewick.

The Elizabethan house is now a diocesan retreat and conference centre but the gardens, in a hillside setting in the Wharfe valley, are open. They contain many rare plants and shrubs. Nearby is Trollers Ghyll, a notable limestone gorge.

Thorp Perrow Arboretum, Bedale, North Yorkshire. 2 miles (3 km) south of Bedale.

A collection of over two thousand species of trees and shrubs, including some of the largest and rarest in Britain, is contained within the 60 acres (24 ha) of landscaped grounds at Thorp Perrow. There is also a wild garden and a lake complete with swans.

8
Museums

ALDBOROUGH

Aldborough Roman Museum, Aldborough, Boroughbridge, York. Telephone: Boroughbridge (090 12) 2768. *Historic Buildings and Monuments Commission.*

Aldborough was the most northerly Roman town, *Isurium Brigantum.* There are remains of sections of the boundary wall and two tessellated pavements. The small museum contains a good collection of finds from the ancient town, including pottery, glass, coins and metalwork.

AYSGARTH

Yorkshire Museum of Carriages and Horse-drawn Vehicles, Yore Mill, by Aysgarth Falls, Aysgarth, Leyburn, North Yorkshire. Telephone: Richmond (0748) 3325.

An old stone building, which served as a woollen mill and later as a corn mill, has been converted to house a splendid collection of over fifty coaches, carriages and other items from the era of horse-drawn vehicles. A viewing platform gives museum visitors a grandstand view of the picturesque waterfalls in which the area abounds. In its former days the mill supplied material for uniforms for Garibaldi's army and later became a flour mill, in which capacity it remained until 1967.

BEVERLEY

Beverley Art Gallery and Museum, Champney Road, Beverley, North Humberside HU17 9BQ. Telephone: Hull (0482) 882255. *Beverley Borough Council.*

A variety of local antiquities and Victorian bygones are housed in the museum. The art gallery contains works by F. W. Elwell, a noted local artist, and there are regular exhibitions. Also here is the Beverley Heritage Centre, an exhibition on the history of the town.

East Yorkshire Regimental Museum, 11 Butcher Row, Beverley, North Humberside HU17 0AA. Telephone: Hull (0482) 882157.

This is a small museum, in the centre of the town, of a regiment with a long association with the area. Six rooms accommodate a variety of exhibits. One room contains the library, another is devoted to uniforms, and a third has been reconstructed as an officers' mess.

The Guildhall, Beverley, North Humberside. Telephone: Hull (0482) 882255.

The former town hall contains fifteenth-century furniture and a collection of sixteenth-century pewter, as well as ancient records and civic regalia.

Museum of Army Transport, Flamingate, Beverley, North Humberside. Telephone: Hull (0482) 860445.

Opened in May 1983, the museum contains the Royal Corps of Transport collection of army road, rail, sea and air transport.

It is housed in military-type surroundings, in a huge hangar-like building: even the snack bar bears the inscription 'Cookhouse'. The well displayed exhibits range from the shiny, standard-bearing Rolls Royce used by Viscount Montgomery as his staff car in France and Germany and the wagon used by Lord Roberts in the Boer War to a Beaver military aircraft. Many of the fifty or more vehicles are displayed in realistic tableau reconstructions, including a desert scene and another showing well camouflaged wireless telegraphy vehicles hidden in the barns and outbuildings of a German farm. Visitors may clamber over many of the vehicles without incurring the wrath of a sergeant-major. Of particular interest to railway enthusiasts is a section devoted to military steam locomotives and other army railway equipment. One of the most unusual exhibits is the only example of a three-wheels-in-a-row motorcycle.

BRIDLINGTON

Bridlington Art Gallery and Museum, Sewerby Hall, Bridlington, North Humberside YO15 1EA. Telephone: Bridlington (0262) 78255. *Borough of East Yorkshire.*

An elegant Georgian house dating from 1714-20, Sewerby Hall contains a collection of local and natural history and archaeology items. There is also a permanent exhibition of trophies and other items relating to the pioneer woman aviator, Amy Johnson, who was a local girl. The hall is surrounded by a public park and gardens of botanical interest.

CASTLE HOWARD

Castle Howard Costume Galleries, Castle Howard, York YO6 7DA. Telephone: Coneysthorpe (065 384) 333 extension 34.

The cobbled Stable Court of Vanbrugh's historic stately home has been adapted to house the largest private collection of period costume of the eighteenth to twentieth centuries (see also chapter 7).

GOOLE

Goole Museum and Art Gallery, Carlisle Street, Goole, North Humberside DN14 5AA. Telephone: Goole (0405) 2187. *Humberside County Council.*

Displays in the museum illustrate the history of the area, in particular the fascinating history of Goole itself, which became an inland port in the early nineteenth century and a centre for the import of raw materials and the export of manufactured goods from the industrial areas of Yorkshire. The museum has much to offer about the history of trade and its relation to transport by inland waterway, rail or sea. A feature of the museum is its collection of maritime paintings, many of which are by a local artist, Reuben Chappell (1870-1940), and there are frequent visiting exhibitions in the adjoining art gallery.

GRASSINGTON

Upper Wharfedale Museum, Market Square, Grassington, Skipton, North Yorkshire.

This small folk museum, occupying two old cottages and run by the Upper Wharfedale Museum Society, contains many items relating to local history and the farming and industrial life of the area. Exhibits also include old veterinary equipment. The museum was opened in 1979 by Robert L. Crowther, of California, the grandson of John Crowther, a noted local historian, antiquarian and botanist: many items from his collections are in the Craven Museum in Skipton.

HARROGATE

Harrogate Art Gallery, Public Library, Victoria Avenue, Harrogate, North Yorkshire. Telephone: Harrogate (0423) 502744.

This municipal art gallery has a permanent collection of watercolours and oil paintings, including works by Constable and Turner, who was a frequent visitor to the area.

Royal Pump Room Museum, Royal Parade, Harrogate, North Yorkshire. Telephone: Harrogate (0423) 503340.

Here can be found the original sulphur well from which Harrogate achieved its pre-eminence as a Victorian spa. The museum contains items from that period, and others relating to local history and pre-spa days.

HAWES

Upper Dales Folk Museum, Station Yard, Hawes, North Yorkshire. Telephone: Hawes (096 97) 494. *North Yorkshire County Council.*

This museum opened in 1979 and is housed in a former railway goods warehouse. The exhibits consist mainly of the collection of bygones and antiquities from the Upper Dales area built up over many years by Joan Ingilby and Marie Hartley, authors of many books on life and traditions in Dales villages. The collection includes an assortment of items which illustrate Upper Dales life and industry in the eighteenth and nineteenth centuries.

HORNSEA

North Holderness Museum of Village Life, 11 Newbegin, Hornsea, North Humberside HU18 1AB. Telephone: Hornsea (040 12) 3443 and 3430.

Items relating to local trades and the social and agricultural history of the North Holderness area of Humberside are exhibited in period rooms. The museum, winner of the Small Museum of the Year Award in 1980, is a former eighteenth-century farmhouse converted into a museum by an enterprising local doctor and his wife in 1978.

HULL

Ferens Art Gallery, Queen Victoria Square, Hull, North Humberside HU1 3RA. Telephone: Hull (0482) 222750. *Hull City Council.*

Thomas Ferens was a rich benefactor and former Member of Parliament for Hull whose gifts to the city include the art gallery, a building in the Corinthian style built around a central court with a balcony. It ranks as one of the best of provincial galleries.

In the permanent collection are several notable old master paintings, including Hals and Canaletto, and English portraits from the eighteenth to the twentieth centuries, including many paintings and etchings by Frank Brangwyn. Dame Laura Knight, Sir William Russell Flint, Philip de Laszlo and Walter Sickert are other artists represented and the collection of watercolours includes works by David Cox and Peter de Wint. There are regular visiting exhibitions and a permanent gallery containing nineteenth-century marine paintings of Humberside.

Hull Transport and Archaeology Museum, 36 High Street, Hull, North Humberside. Telephone: Hull (0482) 222737.

The transport section contains a collection of horse-drawn carriages, once used by wealthy local families, and early motor cars illustrating the development of road transport. In the archaeology section are Roman mosaic pavements and much to do with the archaeology of Humberside. The building was formerly the Corn Exchange.

Town Docks Museum, Queen Victoria Square, Hull, North Humberside HU1 3DX. Telephone: Hull (0482) 222737.

The distinctive building that now houses the Town Docks Museum was completed in 1871 as the offices of the Hull Dock Company. It has three domes and typifies the elegantly solid architecture and construction of the public buildings of the Victorian era. It is in the heart of the city, overlooking Queen's Gardens, and is one of Hull's most prominent buildings.

The exhibits illustrate the many facets of Hull's association with the sea and shipping. Paintings and ship models range from the prehistoric Ferriby boat to the most modern North Sea ferries.

The collections are divided into sections: one on the fishing industry shows the development of trawling techniques while another is devoted to the whalers who worked in the Arctic and brought considerable prosperity to the city.

One of the hobbies of seafarers was scrimshaw, the engraving and decoration of whale bones and teeth with maritime themes, and the museum possesses a fine collection.

Waterworks Museum, Springhead Pumping Station, Hull, North Humberside. Telephone: Hull (0482) 28591. (Visiting on weekdays only by arrangement.)

The showpiece here is a beam engine of 1876 around which has been gathered an interesting collection of exhibits relating to the history of water provision and plumbing.

Wilberforce House and Georgian Houses, 25 High Street, Hull, North Humberside. Telephone: Hull (0482) 222737.

The seventeenth-century mansion where William Wilberforce, the anti-slavery campaigner, was born in 1759 houses a collection of memorabilia associated with his life and campaigns and includes his books, diaries and favourite Chippendale chair. Adjoining old merchants' houses have collections of period furniture, silver and costumes. This is the oldest surviving example of the prosperous merchants' houses of mellow brickwork which lined the old High Street and is the only one with a garden to the front.

HUTTON-LE-HOLE

Ryedale Folk Museum, Hutton-le-Hole, York YO6 6UA. Telephone: Lastingham (075 15) 367.

This folk museum reflects the life and work of an agricultural community through its collection of tools, implements, household appliances and furniture. There is also a collection of Romano-British pottery and artefacts. In the surrounding grounds, old buildings have been reconstructed, including a blacksmith's shop, glass furnace, sixteenth-century manor house and crofter's cottage, making it one of the leading folk museums in Britain.

KNARESBOROUGH

Old Courthouse Museum, Castle Grounds, Knaresborough, North Yorkshire. Telephone: Harrogate (0423) 504684. *Harrogate Borough Council.*

In the grounds of the ruined fourteenth-century castle, this museum occupies the building which formerly housed the Court Leet. There is a reconstructed courtroom scene and many items relating to local history.

LEVISHAM

St Mary's Museum of Church Art, Levisham, Pickering, North Yorkshire.

The Society for the Promotion of the Preservation of English Parish Churches has appropriately used this lovely historic church to mount an exhibition of prints, drawings and other items illustrating the many aspects of church art, architecture and history.

MALTON

Malton Museum, Old Town Hall, Market Place, Malton, North Yorkshire. Telephone: Malton (0653) 5136 or 2610.

Malton's history dates at least from the time of the Romans, who built a fort and settlement, *Derventio.* The area has yielded many relics of these ancient times, which are displayed in the museum.

Eden Camp, Malton, North Yorkshire. Telephone: Malton (0653) 7777.

This museum in a restored prisoner-of-war camp provides an opportunity to experience — or relive — life on the home front in the Second World War.

MASHAM

Theakston Brewery Visitor Centre, The Brewery, Masham, North Yorkshire HG4 4DX. Telephone: Ripon (0765) 89544.

The centre displays the history of this famous local family brewing firm from its foundation in 1827. There is a guided tour of the old brewery.

PATELEY BRIDGE

Nidderdale Museum, Council Offices, King Street, Pateley Bridge, Harrogate, North Yorkshire HG3 5LE. Telephone: Harrogate (0423) 711225.

Nidderdale is the gathering ground of water to supply the expanding areas of West Yorkshire, a development which has created a new aspect to the area, illustrated in this museum in the many exhibits depicting the life of the dale, domestic, industrial and agricultural, through the ages. Displays include reconstructions of a cobbler's shop and a Victorian room.

PICKERING

Beck Isle Museum of Rural Life, Beck Isle, Pickering, North Yorkshire YO18 8DU. Telephone: Pickering (0751) 73653.

This fine Regency house was formerly the home of William Marshall, an authority on agriculture, who founded Britain's first agricultural college here in the early nineteenth century. Its many exhibits illustrate the life and customs of the rural community.

POCKLINGTON

Burnby Hall, Pocklington, York. Telephone: Pocklington (075 92) 2068 and 2114.

This museum is devoted to a collection of sporting trophies and interesting objects collected on travels to various parts of the world (see chapter 7).

Penny Arcadia, Ritz Cinema, Market Place, Pocklington. Telephone: Pocklington (0759) 303420.

Here is a comprehensive collection of antique coin-operated amusement machines, from 'What the Butler Saw' to fortune tellers and pin tables.

REETH

Swaledale Folk Museum, Reeth Green, Reeth, Richmond, North Yorkshire DL11 6RT. Telephone: Richmond (0748) 84373.

Reeth was once a centre of the lead mining industry, for which Swaledale was renowned, and the elegant old houses around the green reflect the prosperity of those days. The museum contains many reminders of the period.

RICHMOND

Green Howards Museum, Trinity Church Square, Richmond, North Yorkshire DL10 4QN. Telephone: Richmond (0748) 2133.

Richmond has had military associations for a thousand years and this museum illustrates the history of a regiment that has always had close connections with the town.

It is housed in the unusual surroundings of a church. Holy Trinity when used for sacred purposes was out of the ordinary in that it had shops built into its outer structure. When it became redundant as a church the building was adapted for use as a museum to house the regiment's collection of uniforms dating from 1688, medals, weapons and other military equipment. Battle scenes are vividly reconstructed and the medals on display include eighteen Victoria Crosses won by men of the regiment.

RIPON

Ripon Prison and Police Museum, St Marygate, Ripon, North Yorkshire HG4 1LX. Telephone: Ripon (0765) 3706.

Housed in the cell block of the former Ripon Gaol, this museum displays in the original cells exhibitions on aspects of punishment and correction from the seventeenth to the twentieth century.

Wakeman's House, Market Place, Ripon, North Yorkshire. Telephone: Ripon (0765) 4625. *Harrogate Borough Council.*

This house, which dates back to the fourteenth century, was where Hugh Ripley, the last wakeman and first mayor of Ripon, lived and died. It is now a combined tourist centre and museum, which contains period furniture and items of local historical interest.

SCARBOROUGH

Crescent Art Gallery, The Crescent, Scarborough, North Yorkshire YO11 2PW. Telephone: Scarborough (0723) 374753.

This gallery contains the Laughton Collection of paintings of the English School, as well as permanent displays of the work of local artists. There are also regular touring exhibitions.

Londesborough Lodge, The Crescent, Scarborough, North Yorkshire YO11 2PW. Telephone: Scarborough (0723) 369151.

This museum of Scarborough history contains a collection of items which illustrate the development of Scarborough as a spa town and holiday resort.

Castle Museum, York.

The Rotunda Museum of Archaeology and Local History, Museum Terrace, Vernon Road, Scarborough, North Yorkshire. Telephone: Scarborough (0723) 374839.

This is an archaeological museum with material from all periods and parts of north-east Yorkshire, and Scarborough in particular.

Woodend Museum of Natural History, The Crescent, Scarborough, North Yorkshire YO11 2PW. Telephone: Scarborough (0723) 367326.

This house was formerly the home of the Sitwells and one wing contains paintings, first editions and other items relating to that famous literary family, but the greater part of the museum is devoted to the natural history of Scarborough and the surrounding area.

SETTLE

Museum of North Craven Life, Victoria Street, Settle, North Yorkshire.

This small museum records the life of this part of mid Craven from prehistoric times.

Pig Yard Museum, Castle Hill, Settle, North Yorkshire.

This small museum contains items of archaeological interest, including remains of extinct animals found in Victoria Cave on Langcliffe Scar.

SKIPTON

Craven Museum, Town Hall, High Street, Skipton, North Yorkshire BD23 1AK. Telephone: Skipton (0756) 4079.

The museum houses an interesting collection of antiquities illustrating the social, industrial and agricultural history of the Craven area, together with geological specimens and industrial implements. Many of these relate to farming and lead mining, which was a major industry in moorland areas in the nineteenth century.

George Leatt Industrial and Folk Museum, High Corn Mills, Mill Bridge, Skipton, North Yorkshire. Telephone: Skipton (0756) 2883.

This museum in a former water-powered corn mill contains machinery in working order, including two working waterwheels.

TADCASTER

Ark Brewery Museum, Tadcaster, North Yorkshire.

The town of Tadcaster has long been a centre of the brewing industry and this museum displays antiquities and items connected with the folklore of this thirst-quenching industry.

WHITBY

Whitby Museum and Pannett Art Gallery, Pannett Park, Whitby, North Yorkshire YO21 1RE. Telephone: Whitby (0947) 2908.

Early and contemporary English artists and watercolourists are represented here and there are also works by Turner, Bonnington, de Wint and other noted artists. The adjoining museum portrays the history of the town and there is a shipping gallery including relics of Captain Cook, who had associations with the town.

Captain Cook Memorial Museum, Grape Lane, Whitby, North Yorkshire.

This museum is in the restored former home of Captain John Walker, the Quaker shipowner to whom Cook was apprenticed. Cook slept and studied seamanship in the attic of the house during his three-year apprenticeship from 1746 to 1749 and paid later visits to Captain Walker. Many of the exhibits have been loaned from their own collection by Lord and Lady Normanby of Mulgrave Castle, who have endowed the trust which runs the museum.

YORK

The Bar Convent, Micklegate Bar, York YO1 2AH. Telephone: York (0904) 643238.

What was one of the earliest girls' schools is now a museum portraying Christian history in northern England. Within the fabric of England's oldest post-reformation convent are displayed the convent's own historic artefacts and other treasures.

The Castle Museum, Tower Street, York. Telephone: York (0904) 53611. *York City Council.*

One of the finest of folk museums, the Castle Museum is housed in the former Female Prison, which John Carr, the famous York architect, designed in 1780, and the former Debtors' Prison, built in 1705, behind which there are parts of the outer wall of York Castle, which formerly stood on the whole site.

The old Debtors' Prison contains a vast collection of firearms, armour, uniforms and other items of a military flavour, including medals, decorations and regimental silver. In another gallery are displayed costumes from the Georgian period to more modern times, and a large collection of period toys from delicate wax dolls to regiments of lead soldiers. Several of the old cells have been imaginatively converted into a dozen craftsmen's workshops but one, the condemned cell with inscriptions carved by prisoners, has been left untouched, a grim reminder of the building's former use.

The former Female Prison houses the gigantic collection of bygones accumulated by Dr John Kirk over a period of many years. Dr Kirk was a voracious collector of everyday objects which were fast disappearing with the onset of mass production. His collection was presented to the city of York in 1935 and accommodated in the then disused prison, which was converted into a museum. The collection contains fascinating reconstructions of a Victorian parlour, a moorland cottage kitchen, a Georgian dining room and a Jacobean hall. There are collections of measuring and optical instruments and personal items such as fans, snuffboxes and hatpins. In the former prison chapel is a display of fire-marks, police truncheons and old musical instruments, whilst in other galleries are fireplaces, cooking utensils, kitchen gadgets and old farm implements.

Perhaps the museum's most intriguing feature is its reconstructed shop fronts. Entire streets — one appropriately called Kirkgate — have been built and those with a taste for nostalgia can wander and stare into the Victorian and Edwardian shop windows of the frontages, which have been rescued and reconstructed with realistic interiors.

Fairfax House, Castlegate, York YO1 1RN. Telephone: York (0904) 55543.

This former house used by the Fairfax family in the eighteenth century for the social season in York has been rescued and restored by York Civic Trust. It is a classic Georgian town house, one of the finest examples in Britain, and its interior has been furnished with one of the best collections of mid eighteenth-century clocks and furniture, left to the Trust by the late Noel Terry, of the chocolate firm, who was also the Trust's treasurer.

Jorvic Viking Centre, Coppergate, York.

Opened in April 1984, the Jorvic Viking Centre of York Archaeological Trust is a new concept in museums, using the most modern techniques to effect its historic presentation of life in Viking York, on the site of the excavations in Coppergate which revealed much about the period. Futuristic 'time cars' carry visitors along a time tunnel while through a collage of sights and sounds they are conditioned for their emergence into a realistic reconstruction of a Viking town, using the knowledge gained of the way of life and industry of the Vikings during the excavations. At the end visitors can inspect the many artefacts unearthed during the excavations.

National Railway Museum, Leeman Road, York YO2 4XJ. Telephone: York (0904) 21261. *Department of Education and Science.*

The opening of the National Railway Museum in 1975 was the culmination of fifty years of discussion and argument. The very first railway museum in Britain, where the railway was pioneered, opened in York in 1927. Individual companies had assembled material; there was an important collection of rail relics at the Science Museum in London and other exhibits in museums elsewhere. After the nationalisation of the railways in 1947 transport museums were established at Clapham, Swindon and Glasgow. As they became crammed with objects, the need for a national museum was realised: its location aroused much debate and eventually a site in York in a former locomotive depot was

RIGHT: *St Mary's Heritage Centre, York.*

chosen. York was an appropriate location: the largest of three historic cathedral cities that were also important rail centres (Peterborough and Carlisle are the others) and a city in which the so-called 'Railway King', George Hudson, had built up his empire in the great Victorian expansion of rail travel.

The first national museum to be set up in provincial England, the Railway Museum is conveniently placed only ten minutes' walk from the railway station or ¾ mile (1200 m) from the centre of York. It has a main hall, with two turntables; on one of these twenty-four tracks converge, on which are displayed locomotives, while the other has twenty tracks, on which carriages and wagons are on show. A long gallery along the whole of one side displays a mass of railwayana.

The collection covers both passenger and freight locomotives and all methods of propulsion are represented. Probably the most celebrated locomotive in the museum is *Mallard,* which holds the world record for steam traction of 126 miles an hour (203 km/h), achieved in 1938, and of particular interest is the collection of royal coaches with their sumptuous interiors, especially the one used by Queen Victoria from 1869 until her death.

The museum has about ninety locomotives in its collection, of which not more than twenty-five are displayed at one time. There are, therefore, changes in the displays from time to time.

The long gallery is divided into two parts. One portrays the history of railways as a continuous theme up to the present day; the other contains items which describe the pre-nationalisation days of private railway companies, with their particular eccentricities. Finally, there is a section on railway steamships.

The Prince of Wales's Own Regiment of Yorkshire Museum, Imphal Barracks, Fulford Road, York YO1 4HD. Telephone: York (0904) 59811 extension 2366.

This is the regimental museum of the old West Yorkshire Regiment and the Prince of Wales's Own Section.

York City Art Gallery, Exhibition Square, York YO1 2EW. Telephone: York (0904) 23839. *York City Council.*

This municipal art gallery, built in 1879, has a fine collection of European and British paintings from the fourteenth century to the present. Included are the Lycett Green Collection of over 120 old masters, works by York artists, particularly William Etty (1787-1849), and watercolours and prints, mostly of local views.

Yorkshire Museum, Museum Gardens, York YO1 2DR. Telephone: York (0904) 29745. *North Yorkshire County Council.*

In the gardens, the grounds of a former abbey, are Roman and medieval ruins. The museum, situated in a neo-classical building with a fine portico, contains a large collection of important archaeological, natural history and geological material and pottery from Yorkshire and elsewhere. Finds from Roman York include a statue of Mars. Other archaeological material is displayed in a separate museum in the Hospitium, the sixteenth-century guest house of the old abbey.

Yorkshire Museum of Farming, Murtonpark, Murton, York YO1 3UF. Telephone: York (0904) 489966.

Outdoor exhibits and the use of up-to-date display techniques indoors effectively illustrate the changes that farming in Yorkshire has undergone over the centuries. Farm animals and frequent craft demonstrations add to the atmosphere.

The York Story, Heritage Centre, Castle Gate, York. Telephone: York (0904) 28632.

The Heritage Centre was created in 1975 in the former St Mary's church. Audio-visual units and films augment the exhibits in interpreting the social and architectural history of York.

9
Other places to visit

RAILWAYS

North Yorkshire Moors Railway, Pickering, North Yorkshire. Telephone: Pickering (0751) 72508.

Pickering is the southern terminus of the North Yorkshire Moors Railway; the northern terminus is at Grosmont, where it links with the British Rail line from Middlesbrough to Whitby. It is one of the longest privately operated railways in Britain — a distance of 18 miles (29 km) — and there are intermediate stations at Goathland and Levisham. The railway, part of the former Pickering to Whitby line, was one of the casualties of the Beeching cuts in 1965 but the section between Pickering and Grosmont, which passes through some of the finest scenery in North Yorkshire, was restored by volunteers, reopened in 1973 and is now operated successfully with steam locomotives and a diesel railbus by a preservation trust. The original line was one of the earliest of the smaller railways of the period of railway mania. It was designed by George Stephenson and from Grosmont to Goathland, by way of Beck Hole, there is a 3½ mile (6 km) long historical railway trail along the track of Stephenson's original line.

Settle and Carlisle Railway (British Rail). One of the most spectacular achievements of railway engineering is the Settle to Carlisle railway, which runs through the territory of the Three Peaks and traverses the moorland above Ingleton. It crosses a majestic viaduct of twenty-four arches at Ribblehead and disappears into a tunnel beneath Blea Moor. The line was opened to traffic in 1876 and is still operating, although there are threats to its future. The weather, particularly rain, has taken its toll of the viaduct and enormous sums have been spent on repairs, but, according to railway engineers, it is deteriorating faster than it can be repaired.

Yorkshire Dales Railway, Embsay Station, Embsay, Skipton, North Yorkshire. Telephone: Skipton (0756) 4727.

Steam trains are operated on a 1 mile (1.6 km) section of the old Skipton to Ilkley branch line.

COUNTRY PARKS

Apart from country parks in the grounds of large country houses (see chapter 7), there are a number of purpose-built leisure parks with attractions aimed at family entertainment.

Flamingoland, Kirby Misperton, Malton, North Yorkshire. This covers 150 acres (60 ha), part of which is a zoo, with dolphin shows, a model railway and a fairground among its entertainments.

Lightwater Valley, Ripon, North Yorkshire. 3 miles (5 km) from Ripon on the A6108 road to Masham. There are all manner of games, sports and rides available, free after payment of the admission charge, together with adventure playgrounds to keep the children amused.

Another country park with entertainment is at **Hornsea**, North Humberside, adjoining Hornsea Pottery. A country park of a more tranquil nature is that of **Studley Royal**, near Ripon, which adjoins Fountains Abbey (chapter 5).

Adjacent to the Humber Bridge at Hessle is the **Humber Bridge Country Park,** where a former chalk quarry has been transformed with woodland walks and meadows and picturesque water areas, picnic provision and play equipment for children. One of its features is Cliff Mill, a windmill formerly used in the crushing of chalk, which is believed to date from about 1810.

Kinderland, Burniston Road, Scarborough, is a play park for children up to fourteen years (and their parents) with water-chute, boating lake and traditional fun activities.

BATTLEFIELDS

Within the Plain of York are several famous battlefields: **Marston Moor**, on the road to York at Long Marston, where Cromwell's victory in 1644 was the turning point in the Civil War; **Towton**, which saw a Yorkist victory in 1461 during the Wars of the Roses, where about a mile from the village on the B1217 road a stone cross marks the scene of the battle: and **Stamford Bridge**, to the east of York, which was the scene of a famous battle in 1066 in which King Harold won a victory against his Norwegian namesake and his invaders, after which Harold marched south to be defeated and killed at the Battle of Hastings.

OTHER FEATURES

Devil's Arrows. In a field to the west of Boroughbridge and visible from the main A1 road are three large monoliths, contemporaries of Stonehenge, known as the Devil's Arrows. They stand in a line spaced well apart and are 18 to 20 feet (5.5 to 6.1 m) in height and composed of course millstone grit.

Druid's Temple, near Masham. This realistic representation of Stonehenge was built in 1820 to provide unemployed locals with work at a shilling a day.

Humber Bridge. A bridge across the Humber was first suggested towards the end of the nineteenth century but it took a century of talk and promise before the bridge became a reality. The Humber was the last great estuary without a bridge. Once work began it took over eight years to complete the bridge, twice as long as anticipated, and it cost more than three times the original estimate.

The bridge extends from Barton-upon-Humber in the south to Hessle, 5 miles (8 km) from Hull, in North Humberside. At 4625 feet (1410 m) it is the largest single-span bridge in the world.

Cynics have described the bridge as a 'white elephant' — a road leading from nowhere to nowhere. Much criticism has been directed at the high charges for tolls and after the initial curiosity following its opening by the Queen in July 1981 the amount of traffic has fallen below the projected levels.

However, the bridge is undoubtedly one of the world's great engineering feats and architecturally breathtaking in its splendour. It is also an important link in a new motorway network, which has opened up easier access to a vast area.

Kilburn White Horse. North Yorkshire has its famous white horse. A huge cut-out in the turf measuring 314 feet by 228 feet (96 by 69 m), it was executed by a local schoolmaster in 1857 on the Hambleton Hills near the village of Kilburn, noted also as the home of the 'Mouse Man' carpenter, Robert Thompson. The horse is best viewed from a distance but for those who want to see it at close quarters there is a car park at the foot of the hill or they may take a signposted walk from Sutton Bank, 1½ miles (2.4 km) away.

Rudston Monolith. Britain's tallest standing stone, the 25 foot (7.6 m) high Rudston Monolith at Rudston, a Wolds village 5 miles (8 km) west of Bridlington, is thought to have been a religious symbol in prehistoric times. It is situated next to the village church.

Skidby Windmill, Skidby, Cottingham, North Humberside. Telephone enquiries to Beverley Borough Council: Hull (0482) 882255.

The landscape of the East Yorkshire Wolds has long been dominated by the picturesque landmark of Skidby Mill. Black tarred, with white painted windows, the mill presents a splendid sight, particularly when its four huge sails are outlined against the evening sunlight or a wintry sky. It was built in 1821 and is the last survivor in full working order of the many windmills that used to operate in East Yorkshire in the nineteenth century. It continued to operate by wind until 1954. The mill was presented to Beverley Rural Council, which restored it to working order and opened it to the public, who may buy the stone-ground wholemeal flour it produces. Adjoining granary buildings and stables have been used to create a small museum, part of which relates the history of the area's old windmills, while the rest contains nineteenth-century locally made tools for agriculture.

One of the Devil's Arrows, Boroughbridge.

10
Towns and villages

AMPLEFORTH

The well known Roman Catholic public school is housed in buildings in which a Benedictine community established itself in 1809 after fleeing from France. In the school library is furniture by the distinguished Yorkshire craftsman Robert Thompson, the Kilburn 'Mouse Man' (see Kilburn). 2 miles (3 km) from the village, at Wass, are the ruins of Byland Abbey (chapter 5).

APPLETREEWICK

Early closing Thursday.

A straggling old village, Appletreewick was the birthplace of Sir William Craven, who was born of humble parentage in 1548 and became Lord Mayor of London. He was dubbed 'Dick Whittington of the Dales'. He made many local benefactions, including the grammar school in the next village of Burnsall. The cottage in which he is believed to have been born is incorporated in the church of St John. He bought High Hall and had it restored for his descendants.

About a mile from the village, at Skyreholm, is Trollers Ghyll, which resembles a smaller Gordale Scar, and nearby is Parceval Hall (see chapter 7).

ARNCLIFFE

The capital of Littondale, a dale of small villages, Arncliffe is built around a green and has a fine twelfth-century church, picturesquely sited near the river and a bridge. Inside the church is a list of village men who fought at Flodden in 1513. Charles Kingsley often stayed here at Bridge House and on one visit wrote part of *The Water Babies*. The old corn mill has been converted into flats. The village is popular with artists, anglers and hikers.

ASKRIGG

A market charter was granted to Askrigg in 1587, when it was the commercial centre of Wensleydale. A six-stepped market cross stands in the village square but the market here lapsed in the nineteenth century. Also in the village square is a stone which marks the site of a former bull ring. There is some fine glass in the church, and picturesque waterfalls nearby can be reached by a path near the church. The village was formerly celebrated for its hand-knitted products, which formed an extensive cottage industry.

1 mile (1.6 km) from the village is the fifteenth-century Nappa Hall, one of the Yorkshire houses where Mary Queen of Scots stayed during her enforced presence in Yorkshire.

AYSGARTH

Early closing Wednesday.

Aysgarth is noted for its picturesque waterfalls, which descend dramatically in a series of broad steps along half a mile (800 m) or so of river overhung with woods. A riverside walk starts near the main road bridge, leading to Milleham Bridge, a distance of approximately 7 miles (11 km), but there is also a short circular walk from the car park of the National Park Centre.

A converted former mill now contains the Yorkshire Museum of Horse-drawn Carriages (see chapter 8). The oak rood loft and reading desk in the church (see chapter 6) were brought here from Jervaulx Abbey after the Dissolution of the Monasteries.

BAINBRIDGE

Early closing Wednesday.

On Brough Hill, to the east of the village, are the remains of a Roman fort covering 2½ acres (1 ha); permission to visit the site has to be obtained from the farmer on whose land it stands.

The ancient custom, dating back to the time of William the Conqueror, of blowing a horn to guide travellers and huntsmen from the surrounding wild fells to the safety of the village, is still practised (see chapter 2).

Charming old houses are sited around a large village green, on which the stocks are preserved. Nearby is Yorkshire's third largest natural lake, Semerwater.

BEDALE

Early closing Thursday; market day Tuesday.

Bedale has been an important centre, only 2 miles (3 km) from the Great North Road and situated at a junction of three roads, since before Domesday, when it was recorded as having a church and a mill, together with more than 500 acres (200 ha) of arable land and meadow.

The church, St Gregory's, is at the northern end of the expansive market place and consists of several architectural styles; its tower is reputed to have been used as a watchtower during the Scottish raids in the fourteenth century. The belfry contains one of the oldest bells in England still in use: it was taken from the ruins of Jervaulx Abbey.

The charter for the weekly market, still held in the market square with its fourteenth-century cross, was granted in 1251.

Near the church is the Georgian Bedale Hall, formerly a private house but now a social and administration centre for the local council.

BEVERLEY
Early closing Thursday; market days Wednesday and Saturday.

The oldest town in east Yorkshire and now the county town of Humberside, Beverley is situated in the centre of the flat plain of Holderness. Beverley Minster, which is one of the finest churches in Britain, was built between 1200 and 1400 on the site of earlier religious buildings. It is of various architectural styles. One of its more unusual features is the fridstool (chair of peace), which provided sanctuary to anyone who sat on it. The town has another fine religious building, St Mary's church, which rivals the minster with the grandeur of its tower and tall pinnacles. Inside, pillars depict coloured figures of minstrels with their instruments, a reminder of its historic association with the Guild of Minstrels, who built it and met annually there to choose an alderman. See also chapters 6 and 8.

BOROUGHBRIDGE
Early closing Thursday; market day Monday.

The main A1 road crosses the river Ure here. The original bridge was built by the Normans but today's traffic bypasses the town across a bridge to the west, although Boroughbridge remains a popular stopover for travellers and a major boating centre. Near the town are the Devil's Arrows, three gritstone monoliths, contemporary with Stonehenge (see chapter 9). On the other side of the town is the village of Aldborough, where the Romans established their most northerly civilian settlement. The area is rich in Roman remains, including four tessellated pavements preserved in their original positions. A small museum displays other local Roman finds (see chapters 3 and 8).

BRIDLINGTON
Early closing Thursday; market days Wednesday and Saturday.

The holiday resort of 'Brid', as Yorkshire folk affectionately call it, has grown up around the quay and harbour. A mile inland is another Bridlington in the old market town with its fine old priory church and attractive sixteenth- and seventeenth-century houses. The original gateway to the priory, built in 1390, has been preserved, its archway rich in fine mouldings and corbels.

The priory church, once one of the wealthiest of religious foundations, was sacked at the time of the Dissolution, except for the nave, which had been set apart as the parish church. After centuries of neglect it was restored in the nineteenth century by Sir Gilbert Scott.

Sewerby Hall, now a museum (see chapter 8), with its surrounding parkland to the north of the town provides a popular holiday amenity, and there are pleasant woodland walks at the beauty spot of Dane's Dyke.

Burton Agnes Hall (chapter 7), on the fringe of the Yorkshire Wolds, is 6 miles (10 km) away on the A166 road.

BROMPTON-BY-SAWDON

William Wordsworth was married to Mary Hutchinson in Brompton church in 1802. Wydale Hall was the residence of Sir George Cayley, a pioneer aviator, who carried out many of his experiments there, including work on hot air engines and the caterpillar tractor. He was the inventor of the world's first man-carrying glider, using his astonished chauffeur as the 'guinea-pig'. His former house is now a diocesan centre where members of the York Diocese can retreat, confer or attend courses.

BUCKDEN

Buckden is the most northerly village of Littondale. A path from the village leads to

Bridlington church.

Buckden Pike (2302 feet; 701 m), which towers over the village. Buckden is built on a Roman road which linked forts at Bainbridge in Wensleydale with Ilkley in Wharfedale. On leaving the village travellers have a choice of two spectacular moorland routes into Wensleydale.

BURNSALL
Early closing Thursday.
Overlooking the village is Burnsall Fell, where the surrounding moorland reaches a height of 1661 feet (506 m). Every August, since Elizabethan times, there have been annual sports here (see chapter 2), including the oldest fell race in Britain. The village, where a century-old five-arched bridge crosses the Wharfe, is a popular place for day trippers and weekend visitors in the summer. The greensward beside the river is an ideal setting for picnics and games. The grammar school, standing elegantly beside the church, was one of the benefactions of Sir William Craven, who came from the nearby village of Appletreewick. It is now the village school.

CAWOOD
The river Wharfe joins the Ouse at Cawood, where Parliamentarians and Royalists were besieged. It once had a castle which was visited by kings and queens on their journeys between north and south. Cardinal Wolsey also stayed there and was arrested on his last visit. All that remains of these past glories is a gatehouse. The square-towered church presents an imposing site standing beside the Ouse.

CHAPEL-LE-DALE
In the bleak little churchyard lie buried over a hundred men, victims of accidents and ailments during the building of the Settle to Carlisle railway line. A white marble tablet to these unfortunate pioneers is in the church. Another memorial to them and their more fortunate colleagues who survived is the impressively large viaduct at Ribblehead that carries the line across the exposed moorland.

CLAPHAM
Now that it has been bypassed, Clapham has returned to being a peaceful little village disturbed only by the sound of fell walkers' boots. It is the southern starting point for expeditions up Ingleborough. On the way are Ingleborough Caves with their spectacular stalactite formations (chapter 1). Through the village and under the road bridge flows a stream which originates near the summit of Ingleborough as Fell Beck and falls 340 feet (104 m) through Gaping Gill pothole before settling on its more serene passage through Clapham. Ingleborough Hall, now an outdoor education centre, was formerly the home of Reginald Farrer, the botanist and 'Father' of English rock gardening, who planted in the grounds many species of plant brought back from his travels round the world. There is a Reginald Farrer Nature Trail, details of which are available at the National Park Information Centre in the village.

COXWOLD
Early closing Wednesday.
The writer Laurence Sterne, author of *Tristram Shandy* and *A Sentimental Journey*, lived here. His former home, Shandy Hall, is now a museum. The church, impressive with its octagonal tower, is built on a Saxon site. Less than a mile south of Coxwold is Newburgh Priory (see chapter 7).

FILEY
Early closing Wednesday.
Between Flamborough and Filey the chalk cliffs of Yorkshire's eastern coastline reach their highest point and are the habitat of thousands of sea birds.
Built on high ground, Filey looks on to an expansive crescent-shaped bay of pure, clean sands which are washed by each tide. The town has developed from a small fishing village into a charming holiday town, its bay sheltered by the protective rocks of Filey Brigg, over which, in stormy weather, great waves are translated into breathtaking cascades of spray and foam. In its days as a fishing village it had no harbour and the boats had to be hauled across the beach.
The oldest parts of the parish church date to the twelfth century. The church is dedicated to St Oswald, patron saint of fishermen, and one of its windows, known as the Fishermen's Window, commemorates men from the town who have perished at sea.

FLAMBOROUGH
Flamborough Head, with its steep chalk cliffs, juts out dramatically at the northern end of the arc of Bridlington Bay. The powerful signals from its lighthouse can be seen up to 20 miles (32 km) away at sea.
The village, a mile inland, has a noteworthy church dating back to the thirteenth century or earlier. It underwent restoration in the 1860s and repairs in 1969 disclosed a medieval window with leaded lights in the form of a Viking ship.

GARGRAVE
Early closing Tuesday.
In the centre of the picturesque Craven lowlands with their undulating and contrasting landscape, Gargrave is at the lowest crossing point of the Pennines, known as the Aire Gap. Transport engineers have taken full advantage

The bridge across the Wharfe at Burnsall.

of the topography with the result that canal, railway and main road all pass through the village.

GIGGLESWICK

Giggleswick is best known for its public school, founded in 1512. The copper dome of the school chapel, now mellowed into a bright shade of green, is a noted landmark. At the foot of the steep Buckhaw Brow is the Ebbing and Flowing Well, which is reputed to ebb and flow eight times a day. It is best visited on foot, because of parking restrictions on the busy main road.

GOOLE

Early closing Thursday; market days Wednesday, Friday and Saturday.

Formerly in the West Riding and now part of Humberside, Goole stands surrounded by flat countryside with dykes and canals reminiscent of Holland. Indeed, it was a Dutchman, Cornelius Vermuyden, who was brought here in 1626 by Charles I to drain the area: he made a cut from Snaith to Goole which is still referred to as the Dutch River.

Goole is England's furthest inland port, 50 muddy miles (80 km) along the Humber. The port was built originally for the transport and export of coal, although it now handles other cargoes.

The nineteenth-century cross-shaped parish church has a tall spire. Inside the church are memorials to soldiers lost in wartime and sailors from the area who went down with their ships in peacetime.

GRASSINGTON

Early closing Wednesday.

A square, recobbled in 1973, is the centre of this popular and interesting Dales village. Some of its shops are chic and tourist-oriented but away from the village centre are spectacular riverside and woodland walks.

The village has iron age associations and finds of that period are in the Craven Museum in Skipton (see chapter 8). Later it was a centre of the lead mining industry, of which there is still evidence on the surrounding moors.

In the village square is a small folk museum (see chapter 8) and off the square are groups of quaint and well preserved old houses. The old smithy, now a fruit shop, bears a plaque recording that the building was once occupied by Tom Lee, who murdered a local doctor in the nearby Grass Woods and was discovered trying to dispose of the body in the Wharfe.

GREAT AYTON

Captain James Cook, the explorer, went to school here: the schoolroom is now a Cook museum, and there are monuments in the churchyard to members of his family. But the house where his parents later lived was taken from the village in 1934 stone by stone and rebuilt in Melbourne, Australia. Its former site is marked by an obelisk of Australian stone, a replica of one erected at Point Hicks, Australia, where Cook first sighted that continent. On Easby Moor, near the village, is the 60 foot (18 m) high stone monument to Cook, looking across the Cleveland Plain. Great

Ayton is a pleasant little village of red-roofed stone houses, with the river Leven flowing alongside the main street and crossed by white-painted wooden bridges.

GREAT DRIFFIELD

Early closing Wednesday; market days Thursday and Saturday.

Driffield is a small market town at the centre of a large and important corn growing area. The market is centuries old, like the parish church of All Saints, which has one of the highest towers in Yorkshire, a prominent landmark for miles around. It is 110 feet (34 m) high, with leafy pinnacles.

Nearby trout streams make Driffield a popular centre for anglers. In 1772 a canal was built linking the market town with Hull. Much prosperity ensued from the increased trade in raw materials brought in by barge and the export of corn and agricultural products. The canal is now disused.

GROSMONT

The northern terminus of the North Yorkshire Moors Railway is at Grosmont, from where the line passes through picturesque scenery on its way through Newton Dale to Pickering (see chapter 9). Grosmont was formerly an important centre of the lead mining industry.

HARROGATE

Early closing Wednesday.

A concentration of springs and wells with medicinal qualities made Harrogate one of the foremost English spas, providing 'the best entertainment of any watering place in Britain at the least expense', as one seventeenth-century writer put it. The arrival of the railway and the creation by the industrial revolution of a new clientele for the mixture of medicine and social life provided by the spas led to further development and prominence, with a corresponding preponderance of solid Victorian architecture in civic buildings and hotels. Although in the early days of the National Health Service the number of treatments at Harrogate exceeded the pre-war figure, there were naturally fewer private patients and when the Health Service contract was terminated in 1969 the Royal Baths closed and a glorious era in Harrogate's history ended. There has been criticism of the local authorities for their neglect of the town's spa heritage in their search for a replacement role, which they are now pursuing as a holiday and conference centre. In this new role the plentiful legacy of good hotels has proved invaluable.

As a holiday centre, Harrogate is well situated as a base from which to explore the rest of North Yorkshire, apart from its own attractions for the visitor, which include the Valley Gardens and The Stray, 200 acres (80 ha) of open space and gardens. It is noted for the colourful floral displays that adorn all the town's public gardens and even its traffic roundabouts.

A new purpose-built conference hall and exhibition complex was opened in 1982 as part of the town's new era. Harrogate now attracts a healthier type of visitor. You would be hard pressed to find a bath chair in use: they are now consigned as curiosities to the museum in the former Royal Pump Room, but not too much imagination is required to recapture a little of the old spa atmosphere in the Assembly Rooms, where coffee and cream cakes are consumed to the musical accompaniment of a palm court trio. Perhaps the current interest in nostalgia will result in more of Harrogate's past being exploited for the benefit of its new generation of visitors.

The town has a fashionable shopping centre and there are countless antique and curio shops in which to seek a bargain.

HAWES

Early closing Wednesday; market day Tuesday.

A bustling market town, capital of Upper Wensleydale, Hawes is a centre for the manufacture of Wensleydale cheese. Regular sales of sheep, lambs and cattle are held in the auction mart.

In a former railway goods warehouse is one of Yorkshire's most fascinating museums, the Upper Dales Folk Museum (see chapter 8). On the approach to the museum is a ropemaking works, which has flourished for two centuries and welcomes visitors to inspect its traditional techniques.

HEDON

In the middle ages Hedon exceeded Hull in importance as a port but its influence declined as Hull developed. Its thirteenth-century church is splendid and cathedral-like.

HELMSLEY

Early closing Wednesday; market day Friday.

Buildings of a mixture of architectural styles stand around the old market place with its ancient cross and Sir Gilbert Scott's memorial to the second Earl of Faversham, whose ancestral home, Duncombe Park, is on the outskirts of the town, a classical building of local design but strongly resembling features of Vanbrugh's nearby Castle Howard.

Just off the market place is the church, rebuilt during renovations in 1868 but retaining its original Norman door.

In the background are the ruins of Helmsley Castle (see chapter 4) and 2 miles (3 km) away are the fine monastic ruins of the Cistercian Rievaulx Abbey (see chapter 5) and the

Rievaulx Terrace, a half-mile (800 m) long lawn overlooking the ruins and with a temple at each end.

Helmsley is the western end of the Cleveland Way and an administrative centre for the Forestry Commission, one of whose forest drives starts here.

HORNSEA

Early closing Wednesday.

Hornsea Mere, 2 miles long and 1 mile wide (3 by 1.6 km), is Yorkshire's largest natural lake, its shores and island inhabited by wildlife and rare birds whilst the water provides popular recreation for anglers and yachtsmen.

At the well known Hornsea Pottery the kilns may be inspected and the potters observed at work. A country park adjoins, while the North Holderness Museum of Village Life illustrates the domestic and agricultural history of the area (see chapter 8).

HOVINGHAM

Early closing Thursday.

Hovingham is an attractive estate village built around Hovingham Hall, which has been in the ownership of the Worsley family since 1307. The hall was the home of the Duchess of Kent, the former Miss Katharine Worsley, before her marriage.

There is an air of peaceful antiquity in the tree-lined road through the village, formerly the Roman road to Malton, the accompanying stream and the attractively preserved Georgian and earlier houses. The Duchess's late father, Sir William Worsley, was a cricket enthusiast and the Worsley Arms Hotel in the village has a cricket lounge containing reminders of the memorable days of Yorkshire's cricketing superiority and photographs of the famous county players who have exhibited their skills at Hovingham.

North of Hovingham, just off the B1257 Helmsley to Malton road is the National Trust's Nunnington Hall, a sixteenth-century manor house (see chapter 7).

HOWDEN

Howden possesses one of the largest parish churches in east Yorkshire, 255 feet (78 m) long. Its high crossing tower, 135 feet (41 m) high, is majestic and cathedral-like in its appearance. The church, mostly fourteenth-century, is built of fine limestone from quarries near Tadcaster.

In the late fourteenth century Walter Skirlaw, Bishop of Durham from 1388 to his death in 1405, financed much church building in the area, including parts of this church and a nearby manor house, portions of which remain. There are ruins of the former chapter house, which has been described as one of the most exquisite little buildings in England, with a wealth of carved mouldings.

It is a town of narrow cobbled streets, with a picturesque brick and stone market hall in the market place. The R100 airship was built at Howden in the late 1920s.

HUBBERHOLME

The church here, which has Norman origins, contains furniture by Robert Thompson, the 'Mouse Man' carpenter. The George inn, across the bridge, was formerly a vicarage.

HULL (KINGSTON-UPON-HULL)

Early closing Monday and Thursday; market days Monday, Tuesday, Friday, Saturday.

Hull has thrived as a port since the thirteenth century, when Edward I saw its potential and bought the land from the monks of Meaux Abbey in 1293. It then became Kingestown-upon-Hull and received the first of many royal charters. Henry VIII, who visited Hull in 1541 with Catharine Howard, gave the mayor his own sword as a gift to the town, so delighted was he with his reception.

Hull's prosperity, through its associations with the sea and shipping, developed as the town was built around the port. The first large dock was built in 1778: it has been filled in and makes a fine public garden. At one time Hull had the biggest fishing fleet of any port, with more than three hundred trawlers, and from the seventeenth century it was a centre of the whaling industry. Its position as a leading port and its access to the great inland waterways of the Ouse and Trent encouraged the develop-

Hutton-le-Hole.

ment of many other industries and with the decline of shipping and fishing, this has been fortunate.

During the Second World War Hull was the most intensely bombed city in Britain: the centre was devastated and very few of its buildings escaped damage. Much rebuilding has followed in the city centre and there has also been redevelopment in the docks area.

Hull is still Britain's gateway to Europe, or Europe's gateway to Britain. It is the terminal for large North Sea ferries. Some of the old docks have been used to build a marina and others have been modernised to provide deeper berths for large cargo vessels — it is one of the main timber ports in Britain — and container ships and bulk carriers. The port area extends 7 miles (11 km) and comprises six docks, 10 miles (16 km) of quays and two deep water oil jetties.

Many of the old merchants' houses have fortunately escaped demolition, although they mostly now fulfil a commercial rather than a domestic role. These are in the High Street, Hull's oldest street, and include Maister House, which has a fine staircase and notable plaster decoration, Georgian House and Wilberforce House, where William Wilberforce was born and which is now a museum, with a pleasant garden at the rear (see chapter 8).

HUTTON-LE-HOLE

This is a picturesque moorland village where sheep graze on the green and small white bridges span the stream running through the village. Many of its old stone houses, with red pantiled roofs, boast their age on date panels over the doors. It was at one time a Quaker village and the home of John Richardson, a missionary who went to America and became a close friend of William Penn, founder of Pennsylvania. Prehistoric tools and other relics found in the vicinity are preserved in the Ryedale Folk Museum (see chapter 8).

INGLETON

Early closing Thursday; market day Friday.

Ingleton is a centre for potholers and walkers. The surrounding countryside is bleak and dominated by Yorkshire's Three Peaks, Whernside, Ingleborough and Penyghent.

A scenic 4 mile (6 km) walk from the village leads through the wooded valley, across moorland and down the other side, providing breathtaking views of waterfalls, including Thornton Force, which falls dramatically into a huge pool surrounded by a natural amphitheatre. There are also spectacular caves nearby.

KELD

A hamlet named by the Vikings as a 'place by the river', Keld is situated on a slope looking down on the river, with several dramatic waterfalls within walking distance. The most notable is Kisdon Force, regarded as the best in Swaledale.

KETTLEWELL

Early closing Tuesday.

An attractive village at the foot of the fells and in the shadow of Whernside, Kettlewell was once a centre of the lead mining industry but now derives its prosperity from agriculture and tourists. It is one of the gateways between Wharfedale and Wensleydale and therefore a popular centre for walkers.

KILBURN

It was at Kilburn that Robert Thompson, a local carpenter, produced the finely carved furniture which distinguishes many homes as well as churches and other buildings in many parts of the world. The son of a local carpenter, his products are reminiscent of medieval furniture. He became known as the 'Mouse Man' because of his use of a small carved mouse which appears as a trade mark on every piece he made. He died in 1956 and his work is now much sought after. Relatives and others whom he trained carry on the production of fine furniture from his workshops.

Kilburn White Horse, carved out of the nearby hillside, is 314 feet (96 m) long (see chapter 9).

KILNSEY

Kilnsey Crag, 170 feet (52 m) high, is a noted landmark of Wharfedale, its summit having an overhang of 40 feet (12 m). The crag dominates the surrounding countryside.

The village is the venue every September for one of the finest agricultural shows in Britain. As a side attraction, it includes a tortuous race to the top of the crag.

KIRKBYMOORSIDE

Early closing Thursday; market day Wednesday.

One of the busy market towns encircling the North York Moors, Kirkbymoorside is often ignored by visitors as the A170 main road bypasses the town. Those who take the trouble to call are rewarded with narrow, twisting streets and the cobbled market square at the town centre. The church of All Saints, with its dominating tower, has much that is medieval but parts were restored in the 1870s by Sir Gilbert Scott.

KNARESBOROUGH

Early closing Thursday; market day Wednesday.

The river Nidd flows down a deep gorge through the town, which has a number of curiosities, including the oldest chemist's shop in England and Mother Shipton's Cave and the

Dropping Well, where the petrifying action of the water has turned a variety of objects into stone.

Guy Fawkes lived here for a time after his widowed mother married Dennis Baynebridge of nearby Scotton Hall. Blind Jack Metcalf, a noted road builder despite his disability, also came from Knaresborough.

There is picturesque riverside and woodland scenery and a spectacular stone railway viaduct across the river provides a much photographed view of the town.

LEYBURN

Early closing Wednesday; market day Friday.

Situated in the racehorse breeding and training area of North Yorkshire, Leyburn is a busy and colourful market town and tourist centre where several roads converge.

Above the town is Leyburn Shawl, a natural terrace which runs parallel with the valley and which affords magnificent panoramic views of the dale.

LINTON-IN-CRAVEN

Linton is a typically picturesque Dales village near Grassington. A stream which divides the village green is crossed by packhorse, clapper and road bridges and by stepping stones.

Richard Fountaine, a village boy who made a fortune in London, founded in 1721 the Fountaine Hospital, fine-looking almshouses built in the style of Vanbrugh.

Halliwell Sutcliffe, a noted Yorkshire author who wrote several books about life in the Dales, lived here in a house called White Abbey.

MALHAM

Malham is the most visited village in the Yorkshire Dales. Its geological and topographical splendours include Malham Tarn, Malham Cove and the dramatic Gordale Scar, a huge chasm, just over a mile from the village, down which Gordale Beck plunges in twin waterfalls to join the river Aire south of the village.

The tarn, 2 miles (3 km) away, is the highest lake in the Pennines, 1000 feet (305 m) above sea level, and forms part of a nature reserve owned by the National Trust. The nearby Malham Tarn House, formerly the home of Walter Morrison, a rich bachelor who numbered John Ruskin, Charles Darwin and Charles Kingsley among his friends and visitors, is now a field studies centre. The tarn is said to have inspired Kingsley to write *The Water Babies* while on one of his visits.

Malham Cove, to the south of the tarn, is a spectacular 300 feet (91 m) high semicircle of overhanging limestone rock.

A pleasant riverside walk from the village ends at a waterfall known as Janet's Foss, near the approach to Gordale Scar.

MALTON

Early closing Thursday; market day Saturday.

The Romans built a fort and settlement here and there are many Roman relics in the museum, just off the market square. A popular and busy market town, Malton is surrounded by rich pasturage and agricultural land and a number of noted racing stables and studs are also situated in the district.

Nearby is Flamingoland, 150 acres (61 ha) containing a zoo and other attractions (see chapter 9).

MARKET WEIGHTON

Early closing Thursday.

A number of highways converge on Market Weighton, a small and ancient market town

Masham cross.

RAILWAY

standing at the foot of the Yorkshire Wolds, its old houses, shops and inns roofed with pantiles.

Evidence of prehistoric settlers in the form of dismantled chariots buried with chieftains beneath barrows was found 3 miles (5 km) away at Arras and there have also been Roman finds. The church has a doorway more than seven hundred years old and other parts dating from the thirteenth and fifteenth centuries. In the churchyard is buried William Bradley, who died in 1820 — a Yorkshire giant nearly 8 feet (2.4 m) tall and weighing 27 stones (171 kg).

MASHAM

Early closing Thursday; market day Wednesday.

Colsterdale, a small but picturesque Yorkshire dale running along the course of the river Burn, meets Wensleydale at Masham. The market place is surrounded by attractive seventeenth- and eighteenth-century houses and the church, which has a Norman tower and tall stone spire.

There is a brewery in the town, one of whose products, a strong ale known as Theakston's Old Peculier, has achieved renown well beyond the borders of Yorkshire.

Set in beautiful parkland nearby is Swinton Castle, the home of the Earl and Countess of Swinton. Part of it is used as a political training college by the Conservative Party, but unfortunately neither the castle nor the parkland is open to the public.

MIDDLEHAM

Early closing Wednesday.

Once known as the Windsor of the North (see chapter 4) because of the frequent visits of medieval monarchs and noblemen to the castle, Middleham now derives much of its prosperity from the breeding and training of racehorses, although this is no recent industry. Horse breeding in the area dates back to the monks of Jervaulx Abbey (see chapter 5). The Abbey owned vast areas of Wensleydale and the monks bred horses on which to transport themselves around their extensive estates.

NORTHALLERTON

Early closing Thursday; market days Wednesday, Saturday.

With its broad main street, nearly half a mile (800 m) long, lined with shops and offices, Northallerton looks busy and prosperous, as befits the capital of North Yorkshire. At the northern end of the main street stands the Perpendicular church of All Saints, with its crossing tower dominating the building. Parts of the interior are twelfth-century.

There was a Roman settlement here and nearby on the road to Darlington is an obelisk marking the site of the Battle of the Standard, a bloodthirsty encounter between the Scots and English in which the former were decimated by a hail of arrows as they charged the English lines. During the Second World War the town was frequented by Canadian airmen in between their bombing missions from nearby Leeming airfield, and many close ties were forged with the town.

Northallerton was a halt on the coaching route between Boroughbridge and Durham. Now a bypass routes heavy and through traffic away from the town centre, which nevertheless has a busy aspect, being a popular centre for day trippers from a wide area as well as a regional shopping centre.

The county hall dates from 1906 and among its attractions are columns of polished limestone, richly carved panels and Cuban mahogany woodwork.

PATELEY BRIDGE

Early closing Thursday.

Pateley Bridge is a good centre from which to explore the man-made lakeland landscape of Nidderdale, the upper reaches of which are the gathering grounds for several great reservoirs which supply the large industrial cities of West Yorkshire. The views are spectacular and the machinery of water treatment and storage provides a new form of landscape and rural architecture. Much of the history of Dales life and the construction of the reservoirs are recorded in the Nidderdale Museum (see chapter 8).

PATRINGTON

Early closing Tuesday/Wednesday.

The Spurn peninsula extends like a thin finger between the Humber and the North Sea, then widens to reveal the substantial fourteenth-century church at Patrington. It is large for a parish church and compares in elegance to that at Hedon. The tower and spire rise to almost 180 feet (55 m), making it a landmark in the flat Holderness countryside. The town was once a busy market centre for the Holderness area but homes there are now much sought after by commuters from Hull. In the nearby village of Winestead, the poet and politician Andrew Marvell, who was Member of Parliament for Hull for twenty years, was born in 1621.

PICKERING

Early closing Wednesday; market day Monday.

There are ruins of a Norman castle at Pickering and Norman arches and fine fifteenth-century murals in the church, the tall spire of which is outstanding. Pickering is an old coaching town, a role which is reflected in its numerous old inns and hostelries. It was the birthplace of Francis Nicholson, son of a weaver, who became a pioneer of watercolour painting. The North Yorkshire Moors Railway has its southern terminus here.

POCKLINGTON

William Wilberforce attended the grammar school here, founded in 1514, although the existing building dates from the nineteenth century. The charming little market town with its quaint old houses and spacious streets has the Wolds as a colourful backdrop. The church, in which there are Norman fragments, has a fifteenth-century tower and its splendour has earned it the title of 'the Cathedral of the Wolds'. Pocklington is mainly an agricultural market town. Nearby are the village of Warter, part of the Warter Priory estate, where the thatched cottages and greens are popular with photographers and artists, and Londesborough Park, where George Hudson, the 'Railway King', lived before his commercial downfall.

REDMIRE

Redmire is an engaging little village on the very edge of the Yorkshire Dales National Park. The village church is a former chantry chapel which was saved from destruction at the time of the Reformation. There are charming walks and waterfalls nearby.

RICHMOND

Early closing Wednesday; market day Saturday.

Richmond is a market town with a long and strong military association. Above the town stands the triangular castle (see chapter 4) with its massive keep towering 100 feet (30 m) high. In the cobbled square below, the redundant twelfth-century Holy Trinity church now serves as the Green Howards regimental museum (see chapter 8). The parish church of St Mary, which retains some Norman pillars, was extensively restored by Sir Gilbert Scott in 1870 and contains a chapel for the regiment. The Georgian theatre, restored to its old glory in 1962, is the only surviving theatre of its age — it was built in 1788 — still to be seen in its original design.

RIPLEY

Where the roads from Harrogate and Knaresborough meet stands the attractive little estate village of Ripley, once a small market town. Tucked away behind the village amid the trees is Ripley Castle (see chapter 4).

RIPON

Early closing Wednesday; market day Thursday.

Ripon is a market town which grew around the cathedral (see chapter 6), the imposing west front of which is seen dramatically on the approach along a narrow shopping street from the market square. It was founded in 699 by St Wilfrid, who is commemorated annually in a special ceremony.

The town hall in the market square was designed by James Wyatt. The medieval Wakeman's House, now a museum and tourist centre, is also situated in a corner of the square. There is also an obelisk to William Aislabie, who was Member of Parliament for sixty years.

4 miles (6 km) away is Fountains Abbey (see chapter 5). Other places of interest nearby are Newby Hall and Norton Conyers (see chapter 5) and Brimham Rocks, a collection of stones formed into grotesque shapes by the weather.

ROBIN HOOD'S BAY

Early closing Wednesday.

The wide arc of bay takes its name from a picturesque village of quaint old cottages clinging precariously to the hillside on cobbled streets and steep gradients. The haphazard arrangement of the cottages and the magnificent sea views make it a favourite resort of artists, and romantic tales are told of smugglers' activities. Leo Walmsley, who lived here, modelled the Bramblewick of his novels on the village and portrayed the austere and dangerous life of fishermen from his local knowledge.

Erosion by the sea was a serious problem but a sea wall now affords protection.

RUNSWICK

Like Robin Hood's Bay, Runswick is an attractive little seaside village of quaint cottages perched in improbable positions on the steep hillside. It, also, was formerly notorious for smuggling.

SCARBOROUGH

Early closing Wednesday; market day Thursday.

Scarborough has been receiving visitors since the thirteenth century, when Henry III chartered a fair here which was held from 1235 to 1788.

Scarborough's development as a holiday resort dates from 1626 when a local woman, Mrs Elizabeth Farrer, discovered a natural spring whose waters had beneficial effects. So-called gentry flocked to the town to sample the health restoring properties of its spring water: it became the 'Queen of Watering Places', developing as a holiday resort in parallel with its growth as a spa.

Two magnificent bays are separated by the harbour, with the ruins of the castle (chapter 4) standing high on a promontory.

Anne Brontë, like many other visitors, found it an invigorating place. She came here to die, in lodgings over which the formidable

Grand Hotel was later built, and is buried in St Mary's churchyard near the foot of the castle.

South Bay is where the holiday development has mostly taken place. North Bay has a number of attractive public gardens, one of which, Northstead Manor Gardens, gives its name to a device by which a Member of Parliament may resign his seat.

Scarborough has several museums, described in chapter 8.

SELBY

Early closing Thursday; market day Monday.

Selby has been accustomed to influxes of visitors throughout its history. Monks from France founded its abbey in 1069 and armies of navvies came during the building of the two major railways which used to cross here (the London to Edinburgh line was diverted to a new route further west in 1983), as well as during the sinking of the canal which links industrial West Yorkshire with the Ouse. It was also a staging post in coaching days, as its inns bear witness. The river here is spanned by a toll bridge: the original wooden bridge was built in 1791 and, to cater for the increased volume of modern traffic, it was replaced in 1971 by a steel swing bridge. The town has great atmosphere on market days, with its stalls offering a wide variety of items. The market cross dates from the late eighteenth century, having replaced an earlier cross which collapsed. The top of the abbey tower, which is open on certain days to visitors, gives a fine view of the whole town. The abbey is described in chapter 6. Much of the industrial activity is related to oil and cake processing.

A rich coal seam has been discovered near Selby: five satellite mines have been linked to a single exit point, housed in modern buildings.

The grave of Anne Brontë in St Mary's churchyard, Scarborough.

SETTLE

Early closing Wednesday; market day Tuesday.

The busy A65 road runs through this old market town of narrow, hilly streets with old cottages rising steeply from the town centre. Its market charter was first granted in 1249. Looking down on the town is Castleberg Crag.

The town has always been an important link in the transport network and there are a number of old coaching inns. Remnants of ancient Settle can be seen in The Shambles, a collection of old shops on one side of the market square, and not far away is The Folly, a dignified old house built in 1675. It now houses an antiques business.

Settle is also a popular centre from which to explore the surrounding countryside either by car or on foot. There are footpaths which lead across the fells to Malham.

It was the birthplace of Dr George Birkbeck, founder of the Victorian Mechanics' Institute movement, whose name is commemorated in Birkbeck College, part of London University. Another distinguished native was Benjamin Waugh, who founded the National Society for the Prevention of Cruelty to Children.

Exhibits in two small museums reveal much about the history of the town and the surrounding area and about 2 miles (3 km) away are Victoria Caves, which date from neolithic times. Settle lies at the southern end of the famous railway line that runs across exposed moorland country northwards to Carlisle.

SKIPTON

Early closing Tuesday; market day Saturday, but some stalls on most days; cattle market Monday and alternate Wednesdays.

Skipton, the 'Gateway to the Dales', is a busy market town on which the imposing church and castle look down. The church was built in the reign of Richard III and contains many monuments to members of the Clifford family, landowners and restorers of the castle (see chapter 4).

The name of the town derives from the 'sheep town' of old and livestock rearing is an important part of local agriculture. Livestock sales are still held weekly in the auction mart, where as many as eleven thousand lambs have been known to pass through on a single day, and the annual turnover of thirty thousand cattle and a hundred and twenty thousand sheep illustrates its position as one of the largest stock raising areas in the north of England.

The town bustles with visitors and shoppers from the surrounding villages and farms as they browse in the varied shops and larger stores in the busy main street or in the quaint old ginnels (the local name for alleyways) and courtyards. Much of the area's history is recorded in Craven Museum (see chapter 8) in the town hall adjoining the main car park. Some of the narrow courts of the main street have been given an updated Victorian appearance, and some of the old buildings in them have been refurbished and given new uses.

The Leeds and Liverpool Canal passes through Skipton — it was opened here in 1773 — and its waterside walks provide a peaceful haven away from the bustle of the shopping centre. The canal is now a cruising waterway and holiday cruisers and other craft can be hired or moored here. Skipton has another canal: the Springs Canal is a cut from the Leeds and Liverpool, almost as old and built originally to enable the Earl of Thanet to develop a limestone quarry. The cut extends into nearby woods and through reclamation quiet little public gardens have been provided.

STAITHES

Staithes, a colourful fishing village with intriguing alleys and prettily restored fishermen's cottages, is the most northerly village on the Yorkshire coast. Captain Cook lived here while he was an apprentice working in one of the village shops, parts of which have been incorporated in a building called Cook's Cottage.

STAMFORD BRIDGE

Here in 1066 was fought a battle in which King Harold defeated Norse invaders, after which he marched south with his forces to be himself defeated and slain at the Battle of Hastings. In the centre of the village stands a monument commemorating the Battle of Stamford Bridge, with inscriptions in both English and Norwegian.

STOKESLEY

Early closing Wednesday; market day Friday.

With its broad market square, elegantly dignified Georgian houses, ample trees and charming old bridges under which the river Leven flows placidly, Stokesley is one of the most attractive market towns in the North Yorkshire Moors area. The town over seven hundred years ago was owned by the Balliol family, one of whose members is remembered as founder of the Oxford college of that name.

All its attractions may be viewed on a pleasant circular walk from the market place along the High Street and West Green, with its attractive bow-windowed houses, to West End, returning along the riverside on a road aptly named Levenside.

The quiet charm of the town is disturbed once a year on the occasion of the Stokesley Show, which has been held every September since 1859.

TADCASTER

Early closing Wednesday; market day Thursday.

Many of the fine churches in east Yorkshire are built of the excellent magnesium limestone from quarries at Tadcaster. The stone used to be floated in barges along the rivers to destinations including York and Beverley minsters and St Mary's, Beverley. In the middle ages stone from the same quarries was used to produce cannonballs. Brewing is now the main industry of the town.

THIRSK

Early closing Wednesday; market days Monday and Saturday.

The countryside around Thirsk is the setting for the popular books by James Herriot, based on his experiences as a vet in the town.

The pleasant market and agricultural town has a cobbled square from which run little yards and haphazard streets of red-roofed shops, hotels and houses. Cod Beck, a tributary of the river Swale, divides the town and provides pleasant riverside walks, and there are attractive old cottages around St James Green, a popular open space.

In the distance are the Hambleton Hills and dominating the town is the parish church of cathedral proportions, with its battlemented tower.

From Thirsk the A170 road leads to the North Yorkshire Moors National Park up the notoriously steep Sutton Bank, from the summit of which are panoramic views of the landscape. From the platform-like top of Sutton Bank gliders take off from the Yorkshire Gliding Club and hover precariously.

THORNTON DALE

Early closing Wednesday.

Thornton Dale is a pretty village which is a favourite haunt of artists and photographers, who are attracted by the picturesque old cottages on the green and the gently flowing stream beside the main street. The village lies on the main A170 road at a crossroads junction which has been there since medieval times.

THWAITE

Thwaite was the birthplace of Richard and

Cherry Kearton, sons of a local shepherd, who in the latter years of the nineteenth century were pioneers of natural history photography. Their wildlife books are now highly prized and much sought after by collectors. The brothers acquired and nurtured their interest and knowledge as they walked to school in the next village of Muker.

WHITBY

Early closing Wednesday; market days Monday, Wednesday and Saturday.

Whitby has a long tradition of maritime and ecclesiastical history. The ruins of Whitby Abbey (see chapter 5) are on a hilltop site overlooking the town. The abbey was founded in 657 and dedicated to St Hilda, the first abbess. It was here in 664 that the Synod of Whitby, when church leaders first set the date of Easter, was held. After destruction by the Vikings it was refounded as a Benedictine abbey in 1078. The present ruins date from the thirteenth century.

The parish church of St Mary, reached by the agile up 199 steps, is of Norman origin.

Captain James Cook lived in a house near the harbour while he was apprenticed to a local shipowner. Cook's statue looks out to sea from its prominent place on the west cliff.

The Irish-born writer Bram Stoker was inspired by the churchyard to write his Dracula stories and a seat on the west cliff overlooking the town and harbour, with views of the church, is dedicated to him.

The old town contains quaint houses and shops built in steep and narrow cobbled streets. From Whitby jet, noted for its colouring, smooth texture and high polish, are produced beads and brooches.

WITHERNSEA

Early closing Tuesday; market days Thursday, Saturday and Sunday.

The building of a railway line from Hull and a hotel started Withernsea's development as a seaside resort in the middle of the nineteenth century. It now has 2 miles (3 km) of promenade but with its close proximity to Hull it is mainly patronised by day trippers, attracted by its sandy beaches. The railway line has now disappeared.

YORK

Early closing Wednesday; market daily, except Monday and Tuesday.

York is the pre-eminent historic city of Britain, a city of many influences, which can be traced in its fine buildings. What is not exposed outside is preserved in the city's multiplicity of excellent museums (see chapter 8).

The Minster (see chapter 6) dominates and fine views of it and the city at large can be seen from the top of the early thirteenth-century Clifford's Tower (chapter 4), which stands on a mound near the Castle Museum. There is much evidence of all periods of the town's history — from the *Eboracum* of the Romans, Saxon *Eoforwic* and Viking *Jorvic*, to medieval times when it was the second city in England, then through a period of decline in Tudor times, to its re-establishment in the Georgian period as a fashionable social centre, the development of the railways and the confectionery industry, and in modern times the establishment in 1963 of a university. York today is an amalgam of past ages.

It has eighteen medieval churches, not all of which are now used for worship, fascinating alleys of shops, of which The Shambles is perhaps best known, and miles of interesting walks varying from the old city walls to the picturesque riverside.

The medieval wall extends about 3 miles (5 km) round the city and takes about two hours to walk, although it can be undertaken in smaller sections. The wall dates from the thirteenth century and stands on an earth rampart built by Anglo-Danish kings and extended by the Normans. A clockwise route starting at Lendal Tower, a riverside defensive tower rebuilt in the nineteenth century and which used to house the engine that pumped the city water supply, takes the visitors past the entrance to Museum Gardens, the grounds of the Yorkshire Museum in which are the ruins of St Mary's Abbey, a Benedictine monastery, the medieval St Leonard's Hospital and the Multangular Tower, a medieval superstructure on a Roman base inside which can be seen chisel marks of Roman masons. Parts of the Roman city wall can be seen here. The first section on which it is possible to walk on top of the wall is at Bootham Bar, which has an early Norman outer archway and part of the original portcullis. From here along Lord Mayor's Walk to Monk Bar there are excellent views of the Minster. Monk Bar is the finest of the medieval gateways. The walk between here and Layerthorpe Bridge passes the remains of the Roman corner tower adjoining the Merchant Taylors' Hall. There is a gap between the bridge and the Red Tower, which is the only substantial brick-built part of the wall. Next come Walmgate Bar, the only town gate left in England, Fishergate Bar, a minor gateway, and the Postern Tower, from which again there are good views of the Minster. Part of the outer wall of York Castle remains behind the Castle Museum and a stretch of wall protected the gap between the castle and the Ouse running from Tower Street along the edge of St George's Gardens to Davy Tower on the riverbank. Baile Hill is an artificial mound on top of which originally stood a wooden tower, twin to that on Clifford's Tower across the river. Birchdaughter Tower is a corner tower and the walk continues to Victoria Bar, a nineteenth-century gateway. Severed heads of traitors were displayed at Micklegate Bar, which has a Norman archway, and Toft Tower is another corner tower. The wall here looks down on a burial ground, in front of the Royal York Hotel, where victims of a cholera epidemic in 1832 were laid to rest. Of the two riverside towers North Street Postern Tower contains more original work and leads back to Lendal Bridge.

Within the city centre, a suggested walk might be taken from the Minster along Chapter House Street, where there is the Treasurer's House (see chapter 7), then by College Street to Goodramgate, in which stands Holy Trinity Church, one of York's most interesting churches, built between 1250 and 1500, with fine wooden box pews and much ancient stained glass. The church is not now much used but is preserved for its historic interest. From the church proceed to King's Square, a small but attractive open space which leads to The Shambles, a narrow street of shops with overhanging upper storeys which almost touch. Down Fossgate is the Merchant Adventurers' Hall, headquarters of one of the most influential guilds of medieval York. By way of Piccadilly, a shopping street, the Castle Museum (see chapter 8) and Clifford's Tower (chapter 4) are reached. Proceed along Tower Street and Clifford Street, another of the main shopping streets, to St Helen's Square, where is the Mansion House, the official residence of the Lord Mayor of York, built between 1725 and 1730. Here also is the Guildhall, a restoration opened in 1960 of the fifteenth-century Commonhall, which was destroyed in an air raid in 1942. At the opposite side of the square is the fourteenth-century St Helen's church, formerly the guild church of medieval glass painters and now the civic church where the Lord Mayor and Corporation attend in state every year for harvest thanksgiving. Off the square runs Stonegate, up which all the stone used in the building of the Minster was transported, and now renowned for its old established antique and silver shops. An alleyway off Stonegate leads to the Twelfth Century House, the restored remnant of a Norman house. Stonegate leads into Petergate, opposite which is the Minster.

The street plan of York does not lend itself easily to the devising of circular walks and the suggested walk above covers only a few of York's historic buildings. Like the traveller to Rome, the visitor to York should be prepared to digress from his planned route as the sight of a building or a street takes his fancy.

On the city outskirts at Heslington is a modern development, the University of York, opened in 1963, with new buildings set around an artificial lake and the administrative offices in Heslington Hall, an Elizabethan mansion rebuilt in the nineteenth century. The university is regarded, visually, as one of the most successful of the new universities.

Where the racecourse now is on the city outskirts on the Tadcaster road the Tyburn used to stand. It was a gallows, where many executions took place, including those of Catholic martyrs, who are commemorated by a plaque, and Dick Turpin. It stood on what was then common pasture known as Knavesmire. Race meetings have been held there since 1731.

Monk Bar, York.

NORTH YORKSHIRE AND NORTH HUMBERSI

E Traditional or annual event or custom

▲ Historic house / Garden open to the public

* Other site of interest

■ Town / Village of special interest

● Other place